The American History Series

SERIES EDITORS

John Hope Franklin, *Duke University*

Abraham S. Eisenstadt, *Brooklyn College*

Arthur S. Link
Princeton University
GENERAL EDITOR FOR HISTORY

Michael Perman
UNIVERSITY OF ILLINOIS AT CHICAGO

Emancipation and Reconstruction

1862–1879

HARLAN DAVIDSON, INC.
ARLINGTON HEIGHTS, ILLINOIS 60004

Library of Congress Cataloging-in-Publication Data

Perman, Michael.
    Emancipation and Reconstruction, 1862–1879.

    (The American history series)
    Bibliography: p.
    Includes index.
    1. Slavery—United States—Emancipation. 2. Afro-
Americans—History—To 1863. 3. Afro-Americans—History—
1863–1877. 4. Reconstruction.   I. Title. II. Series:
American history series (Arlington Heights, Ill.)
E453.P47   1987   973.7′14   86-19889
ISBN 0-88295-836-4

Cover illustration: Planting sweet potatoes, James Hopkinson's
plantation, Edisto Island, South Carolina, 1862. Courtesy of The
New-York Historical Society, New York City.

Manufactured in the United States of America
      93 92   EB   4 5 6

To John Hope Franklin

FOREWORD

Every generation writes its own history, for the reason that it sees the past in the foreshortened perspective of its own experience. This has certainly been true of the writing of American history. The practical aim of our historiography is to offer us a more certain sense of where we are going by helping us understand the road we took in getting where we are. If the substance and nature of our historical writing is changing, it is precisely because our own generation is redefining its direction, much as the generation that preceded us redefined theirs. We are seeking a newer direction, because we are facing new problems, changing our values and premises, and shaping new institutions to meet new needs. Thus, the vitality of the present inspires the vitality of our writing about our past. Today's scholars are hard at work reconsidering every major field of our history: its politics, diplomacy, economy, society, mores, values, sexuality, and status, ethnic, and race relations. No less significantly, our scholars are using newer modes of investigation to probe the ever-expanding domain of the American past.

Our aim, in this American History Series, is to offer the reader a survey of what scholars are saying about the central themes and issues of American history. To present these themes and issues, we have invited scholars who have made notable contributions to the respective fields in which they are writing.

Each volume offers the reader a sufficient factual and narrative account for perceiving the larger dimensions of its particular subject. Addressing their respective themes, our authors have undertaken, moreover, to present the conclusions derived by the principal writers on these themes. Beyond that, the authors present their own conclusions about those aspects of their respective subjects that have been matters of difference and controversy. In effect, they have written not only about where the subject stands in today's historiography but also about where they stand on their subject. Each volume closes with an extensive critical essay on the writings of the major authorities on its particular theme.

The books in this series are designed for use in both basic and advanced courses in American history. Such a series has a particular utility in times such as these, when the traditional format of our American history courses is being altered to accommodate a greater diversity of texts and reading materials. The series offers a number of distinct advantages. It extends and deepens the dimensions of course work in American history. In proceeding beyond the confines of the traditional textbook, it makes clear that the study of our past is, more than the student might otherwise infer, at once complex, sophisticated, and profound. It presents American history as a subject of continuing vitality and fresh investigation. The work of experts in their respective fields, it opens up to the student the rich findings of historical inquiry. It invites the student to join, in major fields of research, the many groups of scholars who are pondering anew the central themes and problems of our past. It challenges the student to participate actively in exploring American history and to collaborate in the creative and rigorous adventure of seeking out its wider reaches.

John Hope Franklin
Abraham S. Eisenstadt

ACKNOWLEDGMENTS

I want to thank, first of all, the editors of the American History Series for inviting me to contribute this volume. I am also grateful to the two outside readers and Abe Eisenstadt for their detailed suggestions and criticisms; the result is a book that has been considerably improved. Maureen Hewitt's editorial skill and her encouragement and patience were absolutely invaluable to me, and I am especially grateful to her. Lastly, this book is dedicated, with admiration and affection, to the historian who first got me interested in the history of the American South and Reconstruction.

CONTENTS

We may not aspire to fame. But great events fix the eye of history on small objects and magnify their meanness. Let us at least escape that condition.

Thaddeus Stevens,
in a debate on the Reconstruction bill,
13 January 1867

Emancipation and Reconstruction in History

In his Second Inaugural Address, delivered to Congress on the eve of the Confederate surrender, President Abraham Lincoln exhorted the people of the victorious North to "strive on to finish the work we are in" and to "do all which may achieve a just, and a lasting peace." Even though the war itself was almost over, its ultimate outcome had not yet been decided. Therefore, the next few years, so Lincoln seemed to be saying, would determine whether the war to save the Union and give the nation "a new birth of freedom" had really been won.

When he referred to the work that had to be done, Lincoln undoubtedly had in mind the two initiatives that he himself had already taken. These were the emancipation of the slaves and the reconstruction of the defeated southern states. If they could both be carried out successfully, then the nation's task would be completed. Unfortunately, however, the president's hopes for the postwar South, like his own life, were soon to be extinguished. For things did not go well once the war was over. As a result, there has lingered over the entire era a residue of disappointment and bitterness. Indeed, historians of the era of Emancipation and Reconstruction have been virtually unanimous in their disenchantment with the period.

This disenchantment has led historians to conclude that, for the most part, the postwar era was a failure. Although they have concurred about its outcome, they have disagreed, often passionately, about *why* it failed. In fact, so vitriolic has been the debate over the causes of Reconstruction's failure that, twenty-five years ago, an article surveying the historical literature on the period was called "The Dark and Bloody Ground of Reconstruction Historiography." Since then, there has been an outpouring of books and articles, but the tone of the discussion has still been emotional and generally critical.

In the process of trying to account for Reconstruction's failure, historians have offered three alternative explanations. In the opening decades of this century, what was known as the New South, or Dunningite, school of interpretation (both terms were applied to the group of young scholars who grew up in the postwar South and were mostly trained by William A. Dunning, the Reconstruction historian at Columbia University) argued that Reconstruction had been misguided and punitive because it had imposed changes on the South that went far beyond what was needed to settle the issues of the war and restore the South to the Union. This view, which became a virtual orthodoxy up until the 1950s, blamed the failure of federal policy on the radical Republicans in Congress who had dominated their party and swept aside all counsels of moderation in their efforts to impose vindictive, uncompromising terms on the prostrate South.

In the 1950s and 1960s, this viewpoint was superseded by that of the Revisionists who claimed that Congress' postwar policies were by no means excessive or punitive. Instead, they were realistic and appropriate. Indeed, had they been successfully implemented and not resisted vehemently by the former Confederates, the changes so necessary for the South in the 1860s would not have been left for the Revisionists' own generation to carry out a century later. Thus, in the Revisionists' view, Reconstruction failed because of the intransigence of southern whites, not because of the extremism of the congressional Republicans.

In recent years, a third view has emerged, and the head-on collision between the Dunningite school and the Revisionists has given way to what has been called post-Revisionism. Like the others, these historians have also been disappointed with the outcome of Reconstruction. But they have argued that it was the men responsible for formulating and executing Reconstruction policy who themselves were to blame for its shortcomings. The Republicans in Congress and in the South were simply too cautious, even conservative, in their approach to be able to accomplish what was needed. Rather than being radical and extreme, as the Dunningites had charged, the Reconstructionists had instead conceived their task in very restricted, limited terms. Indeed, their racial views and political and constitutional assumptions, so these historians argue, were not significantly different from those of their adversaries, the former Confederates. Naturally enough, it followed that Reconstruction failed because it had been a blunt and feeble instrument from its inception.

Divergent though they are, these explanations are all permeated by a tone of recrimination and blame. This suggests a rather interesting feature in the historical literature on the era, and that is the widespread assumption, first, that somehow Reconstruction could have succeeded and, second, that somebody was responsible for its not having done so. As a result, historians have assigned blame to particular individuals or groups for playing a primary role in the era's failure. So the culprits have changed over time, but the approach itself has been one that is essentially judgmental and critical.

This is not the only perspective that can be taken, however. It could be argued that the disappointing results of Emancipation and Reconstruction cannot be laid at anyone's door. Rather, the problems involved were perhaps so far-reaching and so complex that they were virtually incapable of solution. While there may have been shortcomings and failures in specific instances and on the part of particular individuals, they did not significantly affect the eventual outcome. In that case, there is no blame for historians to assign. Instead, there is a need to understand the dilemmas and predicaments that faced the protagonists as they attempted to grapple with difficulties that were daunting and may well have been insuperable.

In this context, the central question is not why Reconstruction failed but whether it had any chance of succeeding in the first place. If this approach is taken, perhaps the period and its participants can be viewed sanguinely and without the compulsion to judge.

CHAPTER ONE

Narrowing Possibilities: Emancipation, 1862–1865

The war was not even a month old when federal troops entered and occupied Confederate territory. On 22 May 1861, a force led by Major General Benjamin F. Butler invaded the eastern shore of Virginia and established a base at Fortress Monroe. Before many days had elapsed, slaves from the nearby plantations began to arrive at Butler's headquarters, thus forcing him to make a decision fraught with immense implications. Lincoln had repeatedly reassured the South before war broke out that the federal government could not interfere with slavery in the states where it already existed. Furthermore, the government had also made it quite clear that the war was being conducted simply as a military action limited to putting down secession; it was not therefore intended to bring about the liberation of the slaves.

So Butler was faced with a dilemma. He felt he could not return the slaves but, equally, he was unable to free them. As a way out of this impasse, he hit upon the idea of calling them "contraband of war." This linguistic obfuscation was ingenious, since it left their status as slave or free undecided, even though they would not in fact be returned to their masters. Indeed, the ingenuity of the definition was so appealing that the president and his cabinet readily endorsed it as government policy.

Although they had not been declared free, the decision to seize the fugitive slaves as "contraband" and not remand them to slavery did nonetheless indicate that, in the eyes of the federal government, they were no longer slaves. Thus, Butler's admiring staff officer, Theodore Winthrop, might not have been exaggerating wildly when he later claimed that "an epigram abolished slavery in the United States." Indeed, throughout the war, federal forces occupying the South would have to deal with thousands of fugitive slaves and would do so invariably under the assumption that they were free. But their actual emancipation had not yet been officially decided and, even then, its attainment was still dependent upon a northern military victory which, it soon became apparent, was neither imminent nor assured.

Circumstances had therefore forced the government into taking actions that it had not carefully considered and that it was not really ready for. This anomalous situation had arisen out of necessity, and it was to be the first instance in a pattern of premature improvisation that was to become typical of northern policy toward the South, both during and after the war.

From Slave Labor to Free

As the war progressed, Union armies took over more and more Confederate territory. In November 1861, the Sea Islands off the coast of South Carolina were occupied. Then, in early 1862, Newbern, North Carolina, was seized. By April, federal troops had entered New Orleans and begun to penetrate the plantation districts beyond the city. Finally, with the fall of Vicksburg in July 1863, most of the Mississippi Delta from Memphis to the Gulf was in Union hands. The result was that a vast amount of slaves and plantation land came under federal control, and something had to be done immediately to provide for the fugitives and ensure that the lands were supervised and cultivated. Whatever action was taken would have a decisive impact on the course of federal policy toward the South.

Of all the occupation zones, the New Orleans district was to be the most important because it was the location for the Lincoln administration's first and most carefully implemented experiment with free black labor. Initially, the military tried to feed and find work for the horde of slaves that flocked into the Union lines, but the numbers were so great that they could neither take care of nor employ them adequately. Consequently, they forced them back onto the plantations which were becoming increasingly disorganized because of the disruption of the war and the flight of both owners and laborers. Since the slaves were naturally disappointed and proved reluctant to return and to work under these conditions, incentives had to be offered. The result was that, in 1862–63, the army took the unprecedented step of offering wages to slaves. Despite receiving payment for their work, the slaves were not free but were still just "contraband of war." Furthermore, their labor was not, in any real sense, free either, since strict controls were placed on their movement off the plantation and they were required to sign a contract which bound them to one employer for an entire year. Further limits on the worker's autonomy were imposed by the stipulation that his employer was to provide food, clothing, and shelter, just as under slavery.

This improvisation was, in essence, a system of contract labor. Its purpose was as much to ensure a ready supply of labor to the plantations and thereby restore order and productivity to the agricultural economy as it was to provide a transition to freedom and self-sufficiency for the contrabands. To achieve the former aim, abandoned and inoperative plantations were let out to government-appointed lessees, while private owners were reassured by the area's military commander, General Nathaniel P. Banks, that they need not fear further seizure of their lands. At the same time, Banks set the hours and rates of pay for labor. A year later, in 1864 when these were increased, they were pegged at nine or ten hours a day and $3–8 a month. Despite this willingness to alter the conditions of employment and recognize the needs of the laborers, the intention, as Banks saw it, was to enforce "conditions of continuous and faithful service, respectful deportment, correct discipline and perfect subordination on the part of the negroes." This was hardly a description of a labor force removed from the strictures of slavery. Rather, as the New England Freedmen's Aid Society observed, it seemed that the general regarded "a *freed* man as a very different thing from a *free* man."

Yet Banks was quite able to defend his system. He claimed that it had, after all, restored order to the plantations instead of the chaos that the northern troops had encountered initially. Furthermore, it had ensured that laborers were not returned to slavery but rather were to be paid by the planters and not mistreated. Banks also reminded his critics that the military authorities had required that the slaves' families be kept intact and that schools be provided for their children. And finally, he regarded contract labor as only a temporary measure that did not necessarily represent the final form that a postslavery·labor system would assume. Essentially, Banks's defense was that his policies had ended economic disorder and fatally undermined slavery.

This was a considerable achievement, so he felt, and he was joined in this assessment by none other than William Lloyd Garrison, the veteran abolitionist. But there were many at the time who were fearful that contract labor was too similar to slavery and that, by stressing the need to restore order, Banks had diminished severely the prospects for significant experimentation and change. Indeed, when critics of the Louisiana system saw that it was also being implemented in the Delta but with greater exploitation of labor and with less adequate supervision, they worried that contract labor seemed to be providing a ready supply of cheap labor for speculators in cotton, while at the same time it offered very little to the slaves.

With the extension into the Delta of the contract labor system, the federal government's plans for black labor after Emancipation were evidently becoming settled and even acquiring uniformity. In effect, this appeared to be the official approach. Nevertheless, it was not the only one possible. Even while it was under consideration, two other alternatives were tried in the South Carolina Sea Islands, and both have been described perceptively in Willie Lee Rose's *Rehearsal for Reconstruction: The Port Royal Experiment* (1964). In fact, the Sea Islands area would turn out to be something of a laboratory for experiments in black freedom. This was because of a special combination of circumstances there. In the first place, all of the former white residents had fled, thus making it possible to reorganize the islands' system of land tenure and labor without interference. Also unusual was the arrival of a sizable group of young philanthropists and missionaries from the North who had come down to educate and uplift the oppressed slaves. Their presence meant that the slaves' own interests would be considered in whatever experimental schemes were introduced. As a result, the Sea Islands offered a far more favorable environment for new beginnings than either Louisiana or the Delta.

Of the Sea Islands experiments, the more cautious was the plan envisaged by Edward Philbrick, a young engineer from Boston. Philbrick felt that he could best aid the contrabands, first, by preparing them for the harsh, competitive world of freedom and, then, by demonstrating that the abolition of slavery was an economically viable course of action once it could be shown that, as Philbrick believed was the case, free labor was more profitable and efficient than slavery. So he bought several abandoned plantations in 1862 and proceeded, for the next two years, to run them under conditions as close as possible to those that had existed under slavery. The only differences were that his black workers would be paid and they would work as individuals on assigned daily "tasks" rather than in a "gang" as under slavery. The latter change was a concession forced on Philbrick by his laborers' refusal to work in gangs. But they were less successful in getting him to raise wages, since Philbrick was convinced that the contrabands should get no false notion that freedom would be easy by receiving rates of pay that were artificially maintained. Instead, he insisted that "all of the laws of labor, wages, competition, etc., come into play" so as to develop in the worker "habits of responsibility, industry, self-dependence, and manliness." Obviously, Philbrick rejected the fixed wages of Banks's contract labor system as well as its assumption that "subordination" and "respectful deportment" were the character traits thought to be desirable in free laborers.

Philbrick's trial with free plantation labor was, however, an evident success. It was extremely profitable, and that after all was what he was trying to demonstrate. But in important ways it actually proved very little. First of all, his experiment was blessed by favorable circumstances that were unlikely to be repeated. He bought his plantations at the government auction for a price that was remarkably low, and he then sold his cotton in 1863 at a price that was exceptionally high. In addition, he paid his labor wages that were slightly below market level. Despite his claims that they were intended mainly to dispel false hopes about freedom, these low wages in fact contributed handsomely to the plantations' profitability, while giving the supposed beneficiaries of the experiment less than they deserved. From their point of view, this method of employing labor and running plantations was hardly a model to replicate. Indeed, it was probably less desirable than even the contract labor system.

Neither of the two experiments for working plantations with paid free labor seemed to offer much benefit to the blacks themselves. In any case, they were probably more interested in obtaining land that they could own and farm independently than they were in working as wage laborers. To this end, serious efforts were also made on the Sea Islands to provide land to the slaves. These attempts would be the most extensive and the most propitious undertaken within the South during the federal occupation. Initially, the federal authorities expressed no interest in making land available for the slaves. But, under constant pressure from General Rufus Saxton, the military commander on the islands who expressed an exceptional interest in the plight of the contrabands, the government eventually relented in 1864 and set aside 16,000 acres of the land in its possession that had not been sold at auction. This portion was opened up for the black residents to purchase in 20-acre lots at $1.25 per acre. Even at that low price, few could buy, and so Saxton urged them to squat on the land, cultivate it, and trust that they could keep it and pay for it later. Soon these hopes were dashed when the government yielded to the importunings of the Treasury department and agreed to sell the land to raise revenue. Once that happened, the squatters were driven off by the new purchasers.

A few months later, however, the prospect of land was revived with the arrival of General William T. Sherman in February 1865 at the conclusion of his march of destruction from Atlanta to the sea. Surrounded by masses of fugitives who had followed his army as well as by thousands of landless Sea Islanders, he issued his famous Field Order No. 15 that opened up to exclusive black settlement the unsold land of the entire coastal area from Charleston as far as Florida. The order provided that families could occupy 40-acre lots to which they were to be granted possessory title. Immediately, 60,000 blacks moved onto the land, hoping that this time they would be allowed to stay. The occupation of the Sherman lands by thousands of black refugees and local residents meant that, as the war ended, the possibility that land might be made available to the slaves was still an open and practical question. But this was not the only question regarding the future of southern blacks that had not been settled at war's end. How they would work as free laborers was also undecided, and so even was the matter of when and how they would actually be freed.

Emancipation and Its Aftermath

It might seem that the question of how the slaves were to function as free laborers would become relevant only after they were actually freed. That was not the case, however, either in practice or as a matter of policy. In Lincoln's mind, the two issues were, in fact, parts of a single problem, since he felt compelled to reassure whites in both sections about the consequences of Emancipation before he embarked on it. First, he had to soothe northern fears that abolition would result in an influx of blacks from the South. To this end, his labor policies in Louisiana and the Delta provided the necessary evidence that the ex-slaves would be quite likely to stay on the plantations as laborers and not flock northwards once they were freed. Simultaneously, his revival of the plantations reassured anxious Southerners that, while Emancipation freed the labor force, it would not have repercussions so immense as to transform the region's agriculture and threaten their own control over the land and its labor.

Lincoln also approached Emancipation with wariness because of its possible harmful impact on the conduct of the war. It was quite conceivable that Northerners might be unwilling to fight if they thought they were being asked to risk their lives just to liberate millions of blacks whom they disliked and feared. It was also likely that the threat of Emancipation might encourage slaveholders, in both the Confederacy itself as well as in the precariously pro-Union Border states of Kentucky and Missouri, to commit themselves more fully to the war for southern independence. Because of his apparent caution, historians have questioned Lincoln's humanitarian commitment to Emancipation. The actual wording of the Proclamation itself has also caused them to ponder the depth of his convictions about this important act. Karl Marx regarded it, at the time, as akin to an ordinary summons "sent by one lawyer to another on the opposing side," while the historian, Richard Hofstadter, complained subsequently that the Proclamation had "all the moral grandeur of a bill of lading."

Despite these criticisms, however, Lincoln did not back into abolition reluctantly but moved firmly, almost relentlessly, against slavery once the war began. As early as March 1862, he presented a plan for gradual, compensated Emancipation. This initiative was seized before Congress had taken any action against slavery as such, since its only step until then had been the insertion into the Confiscation Act of August 1861 of a clause affecting slaves used by the Confederacy for strictly military purposes. Therefore, he may not have been, as he often claimed, about four to six weeks behind radicals like Senator Charles Sumner, and he was certainly never behind Congress as a whole. Indeed, by the summer of 1862, when Congress had passed its second Confiscation Act, which provided for the seizure by the United States of Confederate property in slaves, Lincoln followed immediately with his Preliminary Proclamation of Emancipation. This was a warning that, unless the Confederacy renewed its allegiance to the Union, he would announce the end of slavery within its borders on New Year's Day 1863.

Lincoln's real wishes on this issue are difficult to determine because, in his Annual Message to Congress of December 1862, he had presented a detailed plan for gradually freeing the slaves by as late as 1900 and for compensating their owners with U.S. bonds. It has been argued that this was simply part of Lincoln's basic concern to engineer consent by inducing the southern states to emancipate their slaves voluntarily. On the other hand, some historians have seen this as evidence that he still preferred a gradual phasing out of slavery rather than its immediate abolition. Moreover, since the Emancipation Proclamation itself applied only to slaves inside the Confederacy and therefore outside his control, it has not seemed inappropriate to depict Lincoln's move as a reluctant act, dictated by the grim necessities of war.

Perhaps the riddle of Lincoln's motives can be untangled by recognizing that Emancipation was a risky move because of its possible adverse effect on northern morale and the likelihood that it would stiffen southern resistance. As Lincoln himself later admitted, "I hoped for greater gain than loss, but of this, I was not entirely confident." Yet the president was, from an early point in his career, morally opposed to slavery, and he firmly believed that "the peculiar institution" was the ultimate cause of the rebellion. The question was, therefore, how and when a moral stance could be translated into practical policy so as to guarantee its success. That Lincoln was cautious, even opportunistic, does not necessarily mean that he lacked earnestness and sincerity in pressing for emancipation.

Although Lincoln may have taken a calculating approach to Emancipation, the actual abolition of slavery and the liberation of four million black slaves was a step that was undisputably radical. In fact, the way in which abolition was implemented in the United States made it a more sweeping action than it would be anywhere else in the New World during the nineteenth century. Its most obviously radical feature was that emancipation in America was immediate, whereas in Brazil, Cuba, and the British West Indies, it was accomplished gradually. Also, unlike the others, the American government provided the owners with no compensation whatsoever for the slave property they had lost. The United States was unusual yet again in the number of slaves it liberated at one blow. Four million bondsmen were freed in America compared to the roughly two million that the final act of Emancipation released elsewhere in the New World.

The decisiveness of abolition in the United States can be attributed to several causes. The first was that it occurred as a result of a massive internal war. Only on the island of Haiti, where a slave uprising against the French master-class in the 1790s had precipitated Emancipation, was slavery also abolished immediately and without compensation. A second reason for the abrupt end to slavery in America was that the slaves there actually constituted only a minority—about one-third—of the population of the South and an even smaller proportion—roughly 12 percent—of the inhabitants of the entire country. Finally, abolition was less threatening in the United States because, by the 1860s, the slave population was evenly balanced between men and women and had also become significantly acculturated. These two developments had occurred because the vast majority of slaves had been born there. By contrast, everywhere else the slave trade from Africa had been kept open well into the mid-nineteenth century, even until a relatively few years before each country ended slavery altogether. As a result, U.S. Emancipation would release assimilated men and women, not just newly arrived males.

These differences made America an exception among slaveholding societies in the New World and, taken altogether, they may have contributed considerably to the ability of the United States to emancipate immediately and unconditionally. Nevertheless, abolition was an extremely disruptive and threatening prospect. American whites, both slaveholders and nonslaveholders, Southerners as well as Northerners, contemplated it with great apprehension.

None knew better how decisive and breathtaking a step it was than the slaves themselves. All the same, because the Emancipation Proclamation applied only to areas under Confederate control, freedom did not come to most slaves until two years later when the Confederacy surrendered in April 1865. Still, as the Union forces moved deeper into the South, they became essentially an army of liberation, enabling more and more slaves to gain access to freedom. For each of them, Emancipation was, at first, little more than an idea they had often thought about. Once its reality became apparent, however, there was an urgent desire to experience and feel freedom, to savor its taste and test its limits. The most obvious way to do this was to walk off the place where they lived and discover what it was like to come and go without restraint and without fear of punishment. Moving about was therefore the way thousands of slaves first experienced freedom. When urged to stay with the South Carolina family she had served for years as their cook, one slave woman responded firmly: "No, Miss, I must go. If I stay here I'll never know I am free." Most of those who departed returned soon afterwards, however, to seek work either in the general vicinity, or even on the same plantation that they had left. Many others moved away altogether. Some of them followed the Union army in search of employment and a new start in life. Others moved to towns where it was thought that jobs were more available, or else they gravitated toward the anonymity and comfort of the black belt and away from the predominantly white counties where the ex-slaves living there felt isolated and insecure. In fact, in most states, there was a marked population shift toward the black belt plantation counties and the towns.

Wherever they went and whatever they did, slaves did not respond aimlessly and in bewilderment. Despite frequent assumptions to the contrary, there was a clear pattern and direction to their behavior, which is demonstrated amply in Leon Litwack's *Been in the Storm So Long: The Aftermath of Slavery* (1979). Freedom for the ex-slaves meant independence and autonomy, not just the absence of the most obvious features of enslavement. As a result, they immediately asserted this desire for independence and did so in many ways. Exercising the ability to move around at will and without restriction was, of course, one of them. But there was also the need, constantly expressed, to challenge the system of racial domination intrinsic to slavery. So freedmen refused to acknowledge subservience and demonstrated it by, for example, walking on the sidewalk and forcing whites to step aside. One such experience caused a plantation mistress from Georgia, Eliza Andrews, to complain that it was "the first time in my life that I have ever had to give up the sidewalk to a man, much less to Negroes." In addition, many freedmen changed the names they had been given as slaves, thereby assuming an identity of their own choosing. Countless others defied the norms of slavery by taking the women they had been living with to the military authorities and demanding to be officially married. Once these relationships had been solemnized, husbands frequently insisted that their wives should not labor in the fields anymore but work at home in a more domestic role. Although this probably had beneficial economic consequences because the price of labor rose as a result of the decrease in the number of hands available for field work, nevertheless the insistence by black men that their wives and daughters stay at home had much more to do with asserting male control after years of humiliation under slavery.

Other changes were demanded in the sphere of work besides the withdrawal of women from the fields. Ex-slaves insisted at the outset that they would not work in gangs as under slavery but would only labor as individuals with allotted daily tasks that they alone were responsible for completing. They balked at having overseers assigned to supervise them, and they also refused frequently to raise cotton, with its connotations of slavery. In essence, "No more driver, no more cotton," as one Sea Island freedman put it. Instead, they preferred to grow vegetables and grains, so that they would be self-sufficient.

This insistence that all traces of the slave regime be eliminated received its fullest expression in the demand for land. "Gib us our own land and we take care of ourselves; but widout land, de ole massas can hire us or starve us, as dey please" was how one ex-slave saw it. The provision of small farms or plots of land would therefore offer the clearest indication that the freedmen were in fact independent and, if they grew their own food, could soon become economically self-sufficient. The prevalence of this demand was noted by General Oliver O. Howard when he took charge of the government's Freedmen's Bureau at the end of the war. He observed that many "supposed that the Government [would] divide among them the lands of the conquered owners, and furnish them with all that might be necessary to begin life as an independent farmer." While somewhat wishful, this perception was not just a fantasy in the minds of gullible ex-slaves because the government had come into possession of hundreds of thousands of acres as a result of the war. Moreover, frequent reference was made at the highest levels to the question of redistributing it to the freedmen. Not only were speeches to this effect delivered in Congress, but Sherman's field order proposed it for the coastal area south of Charleston. Also, the Freedmen's Bureau Act of

March 1865 specifically required that abandoned land be leased for three years to refugees, both black and white, in 40-acre lots, with an option to buy. "40 acres and a mule" was therefore not a pipe-dream but a matter of public discussion in early 1865.

The federal government was not the only source for obtaining land. Some blacks tried to buy it. Few succeeded on their own, however, since they lacked the means. What usually happened instead was that prospective buyers collaborated and pooled their resources. Groups of soldiers in black regiments sometimes gathered together enough funds to buy land, while applicants at government land sales often turned out to be, not individuals, but associations consisting of several families who intended to own and till the soil together. Another way to make landownership possible was provided by organizations like the Freedmen's Aid Association that successful blacks in New Orleans created in order to furnish loans and other support to possible purchasers of small farms. These were isolated instances, but they revealed that the acquisition of land was very much on the minds of the freedmen as they emerged from slavery and contemplated what freedom might be like.

No longer the property of others, former slaves now owned themselves. They had the power to make independent choices, and they wanted whites to acknowledge it. Because of this, there was surprisingly little retaliation against former masters through physical violence or through destruction of property and arson. Acceptance of their autonomy, rather than reprisal for their previous lack of it, seemed to be the freedmen's overriding concern. But, to the whites, any act of self-assertion was resented as impudence and ingratitude. Former owners, in particular, regarded this independence as defiance and a threat to their sense of mastery. They could not understand how their former charges had suddenly lost their servility. It was impossible to believe, and even more difficult to explain, that blacks, whose supposed innate dependence and inability to fend for themselves had justified their enslavement in the first place, could have discovered these new notions themselves. Therefore, they had to have been indoctrinated by Yankee soldiers or someone else. But, wherever these upstart opinions had come from, southern whites interpreted every act of insubordination as a sign of impending social chaos or of the inevitability of insurrection. To the former masters, the conclusion seemed inescapable; they had lost control.

The prospects seemed so bleak that many saw no alternative but to emigrate. Others concluded that freedom for blacks was such a contradiction in terms and its failure so inevitable that there was nothing left to do but simply let matters alone. Then, later on, when the social and economic disintegration had become irreversible, they could derive satisfaction from having proven the Yankees misguided in their racial experimentation. But it really did seem hopeless. Not only were blacks assuming airs of independence and equality, but they were also uncontrollable as workers. Since blacks were thought to be idle and pleasure-seeking by nature, planters assumed that they would not work voluntarily. Therefore, when employers continually enquired, "Will the Negroes work?" their question was rhetorical. Regrettably, they felt they knew the answer all along. As one of them concluded, Negroes could not "be induced to work by persuasion." Presumably, therefore, wages or physical deprivation were insufficient incentives, unlike the whip and the fear of physical punishment which had been so fundamental in slavery. Holding fast to their previous beliefs, the planters were obviously as unfamiliar and inexperienced with free labor as the former slaves themselves. As Henry W. Ravenel, a South Carolina planter, noted: "The condition is so new to both of us that we find it awkward to manage." Equally perplexed, though possibly less sanguine, however, was a Georgia planter who asked a friend in October 1865: "How does 'Freedom' work with you?" and then proceeded to answer his own question by admitting, "It runs badly down this way for all parties. No human wisdom can foresee the issue—we are working without data—sailing on an unknown sea—without chart or Compass."

Although both races found freedom a new and untried

experiment, they of course differed markedly in their attitude toward it. Blacks welcomed it, whereas whites resented and resisted it. A few white die-hards refused even to accept the situation, but the vast majority realized that, if they were to remain in the South, passivity was suicidal. Accordingly, they accepted Emancipation but moved firmly, both as individuals and through existing institutions, to limit the freedmen's aspirations for autonomy. So they reasserted the old racial etiquette and meted out punishment for actions they construed to be impertinent. As a result, blacks found themselves more vulnerable than in slavery because they were now exposed to the physical intimidation of *all* whites. At the same time, they lacked the protection which, as valuable slave property, they had previously received from their masters. "Nigger's life cheap now" was the grim realization of one contemporary freedman. Another observed, with a mixture of pride and regret, "I's free. Ain't wuf nuffin." Without monetary value and without protection, blacks were now exposed to the frustrations of a white population that was smarting from the humiliation of military defeat as well as from the ignominy of having their slaves confiscated and freed. The result was that literally thousands of acts of violence were inflicted on free blacks, ranging from assault and mutilation to murder.

Besides individual intimidation, institutional means were also available to constrain the freedmen. Whites dominated the legal system, and they used the courts to curb blacks' newly won autonomy by denying them justice, or even access to it. Later, in the winter of 1865–66, after abolition was officially ratified, they used their control of the state assemblies to enact ordinances, known as the Black Codes, that were aimed at establishing a separate and inferior legal status for free blacks. Although this maneuver was thwarted when the federal military authorities prohibited the codes, the desire to deny blacks equal rights and economic opportunity by law had nevertheless been made abundantly clear. Although they could not restore slavery, southern whites could try to restrict freedom.

In these ways, Southerners, black as well as white, reacted

to the unfolding of Emancipation. But abolition had consequences at the federal level as well, and these took the form
of two new policy initiatives. The first involved the conscription of blacks into the Union army. This would help supply
much-needed manpower for the northern armies at a time
when war-weariness was seriously affecting recruitment. Simultaneously, it would also give blacks the opportunity to
participate actively in their struggle for freedom as well as allay
white fears that they might misuse it once they obtained it.
Black leaders were gratified that the Emancipation Proclamation had included a clause providing for black enlistment
since, as Frederick Douglass pointed out, service in the armed
forces would make denial of citizenship a virtual impossibility.
Also delighted were the officials responsible for the northern
war effort because blacks would ultimately contribute 180,000
men to the army and between 9,000 and 10,000 to the navy
in the last two years of the war. Of these, about 37,000 were
to die, however, most of them from disease rather than com-
bat.

Organized into separate regiments and led by white officers, black troops saw action in fifty-two military engagements.
The most celebrated was the attack on Fort Wagner, near
Charleston, in July 1863. This battle was mounted at great
human cost by the 54th Massachusetts Regiment that was
composed mainly of free blacks and led by its young abolitionist captain, Robert Gould Shaw, who would die in the
battle. Although some black regiments were formed in the
North, the bulk of the recruitment was from those parts of the
South, the Mississippi Delta in particular, that had come under
federal control. But, for blacks who were just emerging from
slavery, conscription into the army proved something of a
mixed blessing. While it provided the opportunity to advance
an individual's prospects as well as those of the race as a whole,
army service also necessitated leaving home at an extremely
inopportune moment. Just when freedmen were trying to consolidate their families and sometimes, as on the Sea Islands,
to grow crops on their own land, military recruiters would

appear and proceed to seize able-bodied men, drafting them forcibly. As a result, a good deal of disruption was caused, giving rise to considerable resentment. This was mitigated somewhat by the record of valor that black soldiers compiled during the war and by the role model for self-assertion and dignity which 80,000 of them provided when, armed and clad in blue uniforms, they later garrisoned the South. Of course, the impact of this on southern whites was rather different, since the presence of blacks as occupiers and liberators served only to exacerbate the ignominy of defeat and Emancipation.

The other federal initiative which resulted from the Emancipation Proclamation was the creation by Congress of the Freedmen's Bureau in March 1865. The bureau was a major innovation in the role of the federal government in America. Through it, the government assumed responsibility, for the first time, for the social welfare of individuals. When the creation of a federal agency to oversee the transition from slavery to freedom was first considered, the notion of guardianship was proposed as a way of protecting the ex-slaves. But abolitionists and the three members of the government's American Freedmen's Inquiry Commission rejected this idea. Noting that the post-Emancipation experiment with apprenticeship in the British West Indies in the 1830s had failed abysmally, the commission's report concluded: "there is as much danger in doing too much as in doing too little. The risk is serious that, under the guise of guardianship, slavery, in a modified form, may be practically restored." Instead, "the freedman should be treated at once as any other free man." So the commissioners recommended that "we secure them the means of making their own way; that we give them, to use the familiar phrase, 'a fair chance.' " And it was this approach, not any kind of special protection, that shaped the Freedmen's Bureau Act in its final form.

The bureau's capacity to aid and protect the freedmen was actually further diminished by specific provisions in the law. The act stipulated that the agency's life was to be restricted to just one year after the war had ended; that its beneficiaries were no longer to be the freedmen alone but all who were in distress, regardless of race; and finally, that its responsibility was limited to only two concerns—the disposal of abandoned lands and the provision of relief to the destitute in the form of food and clothing. Evidently, Congress had decided that the problems arising from emancipation did not necessitate any significant expansion of the federal government's role, nor did the government need to take on any long-term or extensive responsibility for the former slaves. In general, this view of the proper role of government, particularly with regard to racial issues, would predominate in the postwar era.

Had the bureau, in its actual operation, adhered strictly to these guidelines, it would have offered only limited support to the freedmen. But, in fact, it took on responsibilities that went far beyond its specified mandate. The Bureau for Refugees, Freedmen and Abandoned Lands, as it was officially called, did of course dispense relief—more of it to whites than to blacks, as it turned out—and it did start to lease some of the 850,000 acres of confiscated and abandoned land that were in its control. Its most important functions, however, were assumed only after the agency went into operation. First, the bureau established special tribunals so that the freedmen could obtain the justice denied them by the southern civil courts. Then, it adjudicated labor contracts between landlords and their black employees. And finally, it set up and administered schools. None of these responsibilities had been assigned by the law, but, ironically, they became the bureau's main concern.

In its attempt to shield freedmen from injustice, the agency resorted to a number of expedients. Immediately after the war, southern courts discriminated against blacks and would not allow their testimony in cases where whites were involved. The bureau's response was to set up tribunals of its own to hear cases, though these were limited to minor offenses where blacks were in litigation with whites or where a fair trial had been denied by the civil courts. Meanwhile, pressure was applied on state legislators to grant blacks the right to testify against whites. In addition, bureau agents supported freedmen in complaints about unjust decisions handed down by the civil courts. But these efforts were frequently unsuccessful because the agency was understaffed, while its officials were insufficiently sympathetic to the blacks they represented and too worried about upsetting the whites in authority.

The bureau was similarly constrained when it assisted in the drawing up and enforcement of contracts between planters and plantation laborers. Outside the New Orleans district and the Delta, no official decision had been made about how the former slaves were to work and be remunerated. So, in each locality, the bureau agents found themselves involved in adjudicating the terms of labor. With no other model available to guide them, they invariably adopted Banks's annual contract as a way of guaranteeing that a worker would be available all year round. Simultaneously, they tried to ensure that black employees were fairly paid and treated and that they were able to negotiate without duress. Although the laborers were the bureau's clients, agents frequently seemed more concerned about getting contracts signed and ensuring that the plantations were supplied with labor and restored to working order than they were about protecting blacks from exploitation. Furthermore, when freedmen complained to them about the inadequacy of the terms or about a planter's failure to fulfill a contract, the bureau too often possessed neither the manpower nor the resources to conduct an investigation. Nevertheless, dissatisfied though blacks so frequently were at the bureau's feebleness and ambivalence, they knew that without it they would have been far worse off.

In its educational activity, the institution's effectiveness was, however, more evident. Under the leadership of its superintendent of education, Rev. John W. Alvord, a Congregationalist minister and former abolitionist from New England, it assumed responsibility for overseeing and expanding the schools for freedmen that were being established in the postwar South by northern missionary societies and by the coalition of secular agencies called the American Freedmen's

Union Commission. By January 1866, the bureau reported 740 schools in the Confederate and Border states within its jurisdiction, involving 1,314 teachers and 90,589 students. Four years later, these numbers had increased dramatically to 2,677 schools, 3,300 teachers, and 149,581 students. Also, the training of black teachers was undertaken with the creation of about 60 normal schools and a number of black colleges, such as Howard and Fisk, both of which were named after bureau leaders, as well as Tougaloo, Claflin, and Atlanta.

The bureau did not, however, take over and run the schools set up by the freedmen's aid societies. The legislation of 1865 and 1866 that created the bureau and then extended its life and responsibilities had actually given it quite limited power. As a result, the financing of the schools and their day-to-day operation remained the duty of the societies and of interested local citizens. In time, however, as the philanthropists' zeal and money dwindled, agency officials were able to maneuver around the law and expand their role and contribution. Initially, they had merely set educational standards, provided coordination and structure to the loose network of missionary schools, and generally reinvigorated the existing teachers and officials. Over time, however, the bureau generated funds for the construction of school buildings as well as for their rental and repair; it paid a substantial portion of the teachers' salaries; and it worked actively to increase the number of teachers who were black, an effort that, by 1870, had raised the proportion to just over half.

The Freedmen's Bureau actually achieved considerable success. But it would do so only within a limited sphere. Although the bureau's role was expanding, it was still restricted either to assisting activities that were already under way or else to supplying temporary remedies until more permanent and satisfactory solutions could be found. Whether or not its scope could be increased depended, to a considerable extent, on the course that the federal government decided to take toward the defeated South as a whole—that is, its policy on

Reconstruction. This would provide the context and determine the reach of Washington's involvement in the South.

Presidential Reconstruction

Like Emancipation, Reconstruction could not be delayed until after the war was over. The occupation of Confederate territory by Union armies had forced the federal government to take steps toward freeing the slaves from their masters' control. In a parallel wartime development, the army's invasion also made it necessary to consider how to liberate the residents of Union-held areas from the political control of the Confederacy. At first, of course, these populations had simply to be administered and protected by the federal authorities. To this end, Lincoln appointed temporary military governors like Nathaniel Banks in southcentral Louisiana and Andrew Johnson in Tennessee. A more profound and difficult problem was also involved. This was the question of how to create an alternative government to the Confederacy, a sort of government-in-exile, that could be formed in each locality in preparation for the time when the Union armies had to leave. Reconstruction, as this second process was called, had therefore to be set in motion during the occupation, but its eventual purpose was to produce civilian governments in the southern states that were capable of functioning on their own. Thus, the kind of policy that was adopted would determine the shape and direction of postwar southern politics.

Beginning as early as 1862, Congress had debated proposals for Reconstruction. But the matter was complex and difficult to reduce to a single formula. As a result, no legislation had been enacted by the winter of 1863. By this time, large areas of the Confederacy were under federal control and in need of governmental reorganization. Sensing the danger in delaying the start of Reconstruction any longer, Lincoln took action. In December 1863, he issued a Proclamation of Amnesty and Reconstruction. His authority to do so was based on the presidential pardoning power as well as his claim that prompt action was required in response to the wish of so many to "resume their allegiance" to the United States. The president's plan proposed that Reconstruction be undertaken by loyal citizens in each state who could swear an oath of future allegiance to the United States, which also included a clause approving Emancipation. When the number who had taken this oath equalled one-tenth of the voters in the 1860 election, this pardoned minority was to constitute the electorate that would create the new state government to replace the disloyal one.

Lincoln was careful to explain that his "10 percent plan" was not fixed policy. "It must not be understood that no other mode would be acceptable," he cautioned. All the same, it was a specific formula, and he proceeded to implement it with determination and patience. Although it applied to all states under federal occupation, Lincoln selected Louisiana as the laboratory for his experiment in state creation. This meant that Louisiana became the testing ground of the president's schemes both for the reconstruction of state government and for the introduction of free labor after Emancipation. In each case, General Banks was to act as Lincoln's intermediary.

Throughout 1864, the president and Banks labored to reconstruct Louisiana and have it readmitted to Congress. Indeed, Lincoln's very last speech, delivered only four days before his assassination, was devoted to the defense of what he had accomplished there. In these remarks, the president conceded that there were shortcomings, namely that the electorate consisted of a mere 12,000 voters and that, regrettably, some degree of black suffrage had not been required in the state's new constitution. Nevertheless, he urged Congress to reconsider its decision of a few months earlier to reject Louisiana's congressional delegation. Nonrecognition, he warned, would merely discourage those who had come forward at some risk and participated in the effort to create a loyal state government. If persisted in, that course could only "disorganize and disperse them." On the other hand, as Lincoln put it, if Congress could set aside its objections and "concede that the new government is only to what it should be as the egg is to the fowl, we shall sooner have the fowl by hatching the egg than by smashing it."

After all, a lot had been accomplished in Louisiana. Executive officers had been elected in February 1864. A constitutional convention had met in March and the constitution it had produced had recognized abolition, provided for the creation of public schools, and incorporated Lincoln's recommendation that blacks be given the vote, provided they were either literate or had paid taxes or been Union soldiers. And finally, in September 1864, a state legislature had been elected. Yet all of this was now in jeopardy because, despite Lincoln's vigorous promptings, the Louisiana legislature had failed to enact the qualified black suffrage which the convention had suggested, and Congress had then refused to recognize the new state.

What made matters worse was that opposition to the new Louisiana government was arising within the state. This came from two sources. On the one hand were intransigent proslavery elements who thought it had gone too far, and on the other was the radical faction of the Free State party, led by Thomas J. Durant, who felt it had not gone far enough. Beset by resistance from both extremes of the political spectrum, Lincoln's experiment was severely threatened. In fact, the entire scheme would be subverted from within during the months following the selection of Governor Michael Hahn as U.S. senator in the fall of 1864. His successor, J. Madison Wells, allowed the state to fall into the hands of the proslavery conservatives to whom he had unwisely yet zealously appealed in hopes of building a base of support for his dwindling and besieged Free State government. Thus, rejected by Congress and undermined in Louisiana itself, Lincoln's practical trial in state reorganization was turning out paradoxically to be an accomplishment that had nonetheless failed.

Congressional opposition to Lincoln's nondoctrinaire approach was not, however, unexpected. Indeed, it had already manifested itself, rather dramatically in fact, many months earlier. In July 1864, Congress had passed the Wade-Davis bill, which was intended as a more stringent proposal for Reconstruction than Lincoln's. Actually, it was so restrictive that it was probably impracticable. Unlike Lincoln's requirement of a 10 percent minority who could take an oath of future loyalty, the criterion under Wade-Davis was that the process of forming new governments could be set in motion only after a majority of the voters had sworn a loyalty oath, while the actual electorate was to be restricted to those who could swear an oath of past as well as future loyalty, known as the ironclad oath. This effectively excluded all who had supported the Confederacy in any way. The bill also ruled out any role for the executive and the military such as Lincoln and Banks were playing in Louisiana and provided instead for an internally generated civilian reconstruction. And last, the Wade-Davis plan restricted the electorate to whites, making no allowance for the possibility of black suffrage, as Lincoln had done. Offsetting this retrograde step, however, the bill did ensure that blacks had legal rights by stipulating that state laws for trying and punishing whites be extended to all persons and that federal *habeas corpus* jurisdiction be available to blacks who were imprisoned because of a disputed claim to their labor. In contrast, the 10 percent plan offered blacks no legal or civil status beyond the basic personal liberty attained through their emancipation.

When Lincoln pocket-vetoed the bill, Senator Benjamin F. Wade and Representative Henry Winter Davis issued an angry manifesto, in which they flayed the president's usurpation of power. Governments created under his plan were, so the congressmen claimed, simply "creatures of his will," "mere oligarchies" formed under elections called and supervised by the military. Moreover, emancipation and black suffrage were not mandated in the constitution produced by Louisiana, yet leading Confederates could vote and hold office once they had subscribed to a simple loyalty oath. Exactly what the manifesto was intended to achieve was not at all clear. Historians have generally argued either that it was an attempt by radicals in Lincoln's party to undermine his bid for reelection and gain control over the reconstruction process or that it was simply a jurisdictional struggle between Congress and an increasingly assertive president.

There is yet a third possibility, however. It could be that the disagreement was over the constitutional and procedural approach to Reconstruction itself. First of all, Lincoln's policy was clearly a war measure. By providing "a rallying-point," as he once described it, for the loyal elements, he could undermine the Confederacy and shorten the war. In this sense, his approach to Reconstruction paralleled his course on Emancipation, which he had intended as a means of rallying the slaves against the war. By contrast, the Wade-Davis bill was an impractical proposal intended simply to postpone Reconstruction until after the war when the federal government would be in a stronger position and able to proceed more decisively and systematically. The second difference about Lincoln's initiative was that it was conducted on an informal, almost unofficial, basis. Proclamations and letters from the president to General Banks and to Louisiana politicians did not have the authority of law which a congressional statute obviously possessed. Lincoln's plan may actually have been more radical in its recommendations on black suffrage, but that was not the essential point. His entire approach to Reconstruction was being contested, not just its specifics.

With the termination of the war and of Lincoln's life in April 1865, three years of discussing the principles of Reconstruction and almost two years of practicing it had produced neither a policy which was universally applicable nor a single instance of a successfully reorganized state. Instead, Congress had developed an impractical formula and the president had implemented an unacceptable experiment.

The task of devising an approach that would combine the specificity and practicality sought by Lincoln with the universality and consistency desired by Congress would fall to Andrew Johnson, the former U.S. senator and Democrat from Tennessee, whom Lincoln had shrewdly selected as his Vice-

President in 1864. Interestingly, Andrew Johnson would not be the only Southerner named Johnson who was chosen to balance a ticket by a president who was later assassinated. Indeed, the parallel extends further, for both Andrew and Lyndon Johnson inherited an agonizing southern problem which their predecessors had begun to tackle and which they both would take up with alacrity. In fact, Andrew Johnson was in office only six weeks before he unveiled the details of his own formula for reconstructing southern government. Of course, the new president could have waited until the Thirty-ninth Congress convened in December 1865 and let the legislative branch assume responsibility for framing a viable policy. Or, at least, he could have consulted with it before taking any action himself. But Johnson was not about to practice such self-denial. Rather, he wanted to implement a plan of Reconstruction before Congress assembled, leaving the legislators with the duty simply of ratifying his actions by admitting the congressmen that the South had elected under his policy. As with Lincoln's approach, Congress' role in Reconstruction was reduced simply to approving it once it had happened.

Actually, Johnson claimed that he was following Lincoln's example. Like his predecessor, he took a conciliatory, magnanimous stance toward the South. Furthermore, he based his own policy on a draft proclamation for North Carolina that was under discussion in cabinet before Lincoln's death. Johnson also employed the executive proclamation as the device for communicating his demands and, as Lincoln had done, relied heavily on oaths of allegiance for sifting the loyal from the unrepentant.

Despite these similarities, however, there were differences in context and administration that ultimately were to prove more significant. First of all, Johnson's policy was introduced after the war was over when there was no longer a competing claim on the allegiance of Southerners, thus making the oath virtually ineffective as a test of loyalty. Johnson also did not treat each state as a distinctive polity but employed the same approach across the board. Furthermore, he paid little attention to molding and screening the electorate, as Lincoln had done, but simply invited any and all who would take the oath of allegiance to vote. Finally, Johnson was not prepared to adapt his policy to changing circumstances in the South or to the concerns of Congress. Instead, he clung tenaciously to the single formula he had adopted, while yielding its specifics whenever challenged by the South. And this was not the way Lincoln operated.

The two presidents' past careers also differed significantly. Johnson was a strict constitutionalist who, like his hero, Andrew Jackson, believed that government's role should be as limited as possible, especially that of the federal authority in relation to the states. Also divergent from Lincoln's were his successor's feelings about the war. While the former spoke of "binding up the nation's wounds" and bearing "malice toward none," Johnson, as Military Governor of Tennessee and a member of Congress' Committee on the Conduct of the War, had exuded vengeance, frequently pronouncing in public that "Treason must be made odious and traitors punished." So severe did Johnson's views about chastising the rebels seem to be that leading radical Republicans expressed great confidence that the new president would be more of an ally than Lincoln had been. Indeed, one of them, Benjamin F. Wade, claimed jubilantly: "By the gods, there will be no trouble now in running the government."

But the radicals misconstrued Johnson's intentions. His punitive statements were only sentiments; they did not translate into policy. Johnson's plebeian origins and his political identification with the common people may have generated in him a detestation toward the slaveholding elite, but he was no populist radical determined to reduce their power and wealth. No matter what his sentiments were, the new president's instinctive conservatism and his suspicion of governmental activism guaranteed that he could not make the postwar period "a time of triumph for the yeoman class" of the South, as Kenneth Stampp claimed in his *The Era of Reconstruction, 1865–1877* (1965). There was, however, a vague nod in that direction when he excluded from his amnesty all whose assets were worth more than $20,000 and when, in his Reconstruction plan, he added a requirement that states had to repudiate their Confederate war debt. Despite these strikes against wealthy Southerners, Johnson's policy was more conciliatory than Lincoln's. And this realization soon shocked and alarmed the radicals, while it provoked anxiety among the rest of the Republican party.

In two proclamations issued on 29 May 1865, President Johnson announced his plan for Amnesty and Reconstruction. In the first, he decreed that, by subscribing to an oath of future loyalty, all adult males in the states of the Confederacy would be pardoned and able to vote and hold office. From this he excluded the Confederacy's political and military leaders and those worth more than $20,000; individuals from these categories would have to apply personally to the president for clemency. The other proclamation, first issued for North Carolina and then later for the remaining states, appointed provisional governors whose task was to take charge of the reorganization of their state's political life. This they would do by supervising the registration of voters; by calling a constitutional convention to nullify the state's secession ordinance and legalize the abolition of slavery; and, finally, by holding elections for state legislators and executive officers as well as for congressmen. When all of this was done, and the legislature had also ratified the Thirteenth Amendment prohibiting slavery, the state would be ready to rejoin the Union. Then, with the seating of the southern delegations in Congress, an outcome which the president fully expected, Reconstruction would be completed.

Andrew Johnson had moved decisively and rapidly to seize control of Reconstruction. Yet, within a few months, that control had slipped out of his grasp and into the hands of the provisional governments that he himself had set up in the South. This dramatic shift of power had occurred, so some historians have argued, because of shortcomings in Johnson himself. In his *Andrew Johnson and Reconstruction* (1960),

Eric McKitrick, for example, suggested that Johnson's difficulties arose mainly from his ineptness and rigidity as a politician. Another possible explanation, suggested by Kenneth Stampp, was that, deep down, the plebeian president was an admirer of the southern gentry that he excoriated in public, and so he was unable to stand up to their demands for personal clemency and restored political influence. Plausible as these explanations may seem, they do not settle the issue entirely. Johnson did indeed have personal liabilities, but these alone do not account for the deficiencies in his policy. They merely aggravated them. For Johnson's plan was intended to produce the rather minimal reconstruction of the South that was in fact the outcome. The president himself had indicated this when he referred to it as "restoration" rather than "reconstruction." Had it been more firmly and carefully administered, Congress might have found it more difficult to repudiate, but the policy would still have been inadequate. Nevertheless, the president himself was neither terribly surprised nor bothered by what actually transpired in the South, since his aims were essentially being realized.

The president's goal was simply to create functioning governments in the Confederate states and not to engage in any redistribution of political power. He required only a minimal criterion—the swearing of an oath of future allegiance—for eligibility to vote, and he imposed no restrictions other than that same oath on officeholding. Indirectly, he did hint that politicians who had opposed secession in 1860 or been critical of the Confederate war effort would be more acceptable as officeholders than secessionists. And, in fact, all of the provisional governors he appointed had past records that met those two criteria. Moreover, men of that stripe were, by and large, elected to state and federal office under the president's plan. A second assumption in Johnson's approach was that reorganization was to be carried out by the Southerners themselves as evidence of a voluntary desire to rejoin the Union and demonstrate their loyalty. It should not therefore be done unwillingly, simply to meet terms stipulated by Washington.

As the president later explained, his objective was "everywhere to stimulate the loyalty of the South themselves, and make it the spring of loyal conduct and proper legislation rather than to impose upon them laws and conditions by external force." This emphasis on voluntary compliance naturally ruled out the possibility of forceful intervention by the president himself.

Besides not wishing to cajole the Southerners to concur, the president actually believed they would see the advantage of cooperation for themselves. Indeed, there were, he felt, plenty of incentives for them to realize this. After all, by acting in good faith and accepting the president's own generous requirements, they would have a good chance of being readmitted to Congress and of having the obtrusive federal military presence removed. But Johnson was so eager to ensure that his provisional governments were not embarrassed or criticized that he allowed even these stimuli to evaporate. When provisional governors or legislatures complained and procrastinated, he invariably gave in to them. In August, when Mississippi officials expressed dissatisfaction that law and order in their state was maintained exclusively by the U.S. troops, he yielded and allowed them to raise their own militia units. Later, he made no objection when several states merely repealed their secession ordinances, rather than nullified them. The same thing happened when some of them refused to ratify the Thirteenth Amendment and when Mississippi and South Carolina enacted discriminatory Black Codes.

Johnson also yielded the influence he possessed through his power to pardon leading Confederates. Rather than withholding clemency until the petitioner had shown evidence of repentance and cooperation, he granted it wholesale for virtually all of the petitions submitted to him by the provisional governors. Meanwhile, to those influential individuals who petitioned him personally, he was extremely obliging. This was all done under the mistaken impression that generosity would elicit the personal and political support of those men of prominence whose disabilities he had removed. The final indication of Johnson's accommodationism was his failure to point out to the South that, if it fell short of the president's recommendations, Congress would have good reason to refuse readmission. Instead, he acted as if Congress was only marginally involved and was likely, in any case, to admit the southern delegations rather than risk the political turmoil that would almost certainly result from their rejection.

The president's evident willingness to appease southern anxiety was further confirmed by a dramatic, but unheralded, initiative that he took during the late summer while the constitutional conventions were in session. After engaging in a running battle with Commissioner Oliver O. Howard, Johnson finally ordered the Freedmen's Bureau to restore seized and abandoned land to its previous owners on condition that they had taken the oath and been amnestied. This unilateral action revealed the extent of Johnson's power and the limits of his view of Reconstruction. It also showed how much was to be gained from accepting the oath. The shame of the "I am nasty" oath, as Southerners deprecatingly called it, was nothing compared to the wealth and status it restored. Of course, the reverse side of the restoration of their land to the rebels was that those people who currently occupied it, such as the Sea Islands freedmen, would have to leave. The result was the final abandonment of the precarious land experiment on the Islands. The presidential order also made it clear that land redistribution was no longer on the postwar political agenda, unless Congress decided to contest the president's action. In the meantime, Johnson's decision was bureau policy and it was legally binding. Southern landowners could breathe a sigh of relief.

Because of President Johnson's soothing reassurance, whatever constraints on southern political behavior had existed initially became increasingly ineffective, even irrelevant. Unpardoned candidates ran for office and, once elected, were immediately amnestied, while even prominent Confederates, like Alexander Stephens who had been Jefferson Davis' vice-president, were chosen to represent the South in Congress. Of course, Southerners argued that Stephens had been an unceasing critic of the Confederate government's conduct of the war and was, in their view, one of the region's most respected and therefore most eligible statesmen to grace the halls of Congress. All the same, it was a choice that was bound to be interpreted rather differently in the North. Furthermore, there seemed to be more concern among politicians at the head of affairs in the South to make a reputation with the local voters as defenders of the region who were able to stand up to northern blandishments than there was to satisfy the victor's demands for repentance. Becoming increasingly convinced that the president needed their cooperation more than they needed to meet his minimal demands, southern politicians focussed their attention on defending their region's autonomy and strengthening its defenses. In the process, they overlooked the danger that, without their compliance, Johnson's ability to defend his policy, and therefore the South, from the more radical element in the Republican party was bound to be seriously undermined.

This attitude was pervasive in the South by the fall. In September, one of the members of the South Carolina convention, James B. Campbell, reported to the president: "There is a remarkable forgetfulness of our true situation.... The delegates seem not only to rely upon you for their salvation but consider it already secure forgetful that they must do their full share to aid and strengthen your efforts." Yet how could they think otherwise when, in August, after allowing Mississippi to raise its own militia force, Johnson had made it known that "the great object is to induce the people to come forward in the defence of the State and Federal government.... The people must be trusted with their government." What this actually meant—and certainly this was how it was understood in the South—was that the imperatives of Reconstruction had been reversed. Rather than the defeated rebels having to offer guarantees and give assurances so as to convince a skeptical North, it was to be the other way around, as the president found himself trying to encourage wary Southerners to rejoin the Union.

The result was that the Republicans in Congress who had

feared that the president's minimal policy of restoration would be inadequate were given ample reason to oppose southern readmission to the new Thirty-ninth Congress. By a devious maneuver aimed at circumventing the Committee on Elections where claims for contested seats were customarily presented and eventually, after lengthy hearings, adjudicated, the Republican leadership arranged instead for the clerk of the House to omit the names of the southern delegates from the roll call. Needless to say, this was a decisive move. By refusing to admit the South, Congress had, in effect, repudiated all that the president had done to reunite the war-torn and dismembered country.

CHAPTER TWO

Limited Power: Reconstruction, 1866–1873

By refusing to seat the southern representatives in December 1865, Congress had precipitated a major governmental crisis. Only six months after the conclusion of a massive armed struggle to reunite a divided nation, disunion was being prolonged. At the same time, a serious division was emerging within the federal government as the legislative branch challenged the president's claim to determine the conditions of southern readmission.

The situation was perilous. In the South, the snubbing of the region's attempt to reenter the Union added frustration to the existing mood of defeat and despair. Since the rejected former Confederates now controlled their own state governments, there were few checks on them, besides the limited U.S. military presence, if they chose to vent their fury on their ex-slaves and on the Unionists, that is, those whites who had been lukewarm in their support of the Confederacy. Delay in presenting a conclusive set of alternative terms could only exacerbate an already volatile and tense situation within the

South. It would also have a harmful impact in Washington. If the president and Congress were unable to settle their differences over southern policy, the conflict could easily escalate into a constitutional crisis, with each branch of government disputing the other's authority. And, in fact, what was feared actually materialized. More than two years were to elapse before the South was finally readmitted. During that time, Andrew Johnson became locked in a struggle with Congress that resulted in his attempted impeachment. Meanwhile, the South suffered continual turmoil and uncertainty.

The Scope of Congressional Policy

There were two options available to Congress as it considered what course of action to pursue after its rejection of the southern delegations elected under President Johnson's policy. Either Congress could overturn everything he had done and begin Reconstruction anew. Or it could try to cooperate with the president by accepting much of what he had done and then supplementing it with further demands on the former Confederates and with additional protection for the freedmen and Unionists. Historians once thought that Congress was determined from the outset to challenge the president and impose an alternative plan of its own. But now, as a result of Revisionist scholarship, it has been recognized that this was not so. Although perturbed at what had transpired in the South during 1865, the majority of congressmen were also extremely concerned to avoid an irrevocable split with the head of the executive branch who was concurrently the highest elected official in their own party, the Republican. A decisive break with Johnson would, therefore, undermine northern unity in dealing with its defeated southern enemies; complicate the operations of the federal government; and weaken the Republican party which was, after all, only ten years old and still trying to establish itself.

A strong sentiment favoring conciliation in its relations with Andrew Johnson was evident in Congress from the outset.

The Joint Committee on Reconstruction, which had been set up to judge the qualifications of the southern congressmen-elect and to make recommendations about Reconstruction policy, displayed a good deal of caution. Indeed, it was prepared initially to consider a plan for the South that was restricted simply to reducing its representation in Congress. At the same time, its chair, Senator William P. Fessenden of Maine, was in touch with the president seeking his views and reactions to the committee's deliberations. Also, Congress itself was turning aside bolder plans for the South and focussing its attention instead on two bills sponsored by Senator Lyman Trumbull from Illinois. Their purpose was to keep open the lines of communication and test the president's willingness to cooperate.

Besides their strategic importance in the dispute with Johnson, these measures were also significant on substantive grounds. The first of Trumbull's bills extended the life of the Freedmen's Bureau. In addition, the bureau was granted an annual appropriation and its jurisdiction was expanded so as to include those responsibilities it had assumed unofficially, such as the supervision of labor contracts and the provision of temporary courts for the freedmen. Despite its increased scope, the bureau's role was still circumscribed. Clearly, it was not intended to furnish exclusive protection for the freedmen but to offer redress when existing civil institutions failed to treat them fairly. Also severely restricted was the bureau's potential for making land available to the former slaves. Not only did the bill ratify President Johnson's order of September 1865 restoring their lands to pardoned rebels, but it also placed a three-year limit on the occupation of land that had been opened up for black settlement by Sherman's Field Order No. 15. The freedmen's chances of obtaining land were vanishing, as was the possibility that the bureau might act as an instrument of social change.

Nevertheless, it should be noted that Congress did make one move towards providing land for the ex-slaves when, a few months later in June 1866, it passed a Homestead Act specially for the South. Under the astute management of Congressman George W. Julian, a radical Republican from Indiana, the measure, which was a pale imitation of the wartime Homestead Act of 1862, made available 44 million acres of public land in Alabama, Arkansas, Florida, Louisiana, and Mississippi in grants of 80-acre lots to settlers who worked on their own preempted land for five years. The proposal was acceptable to Congress because it did not involve the confiscation of land from its current owners but offered instead simply to open up uncultivated areas of the public domain for settlement by blacks and others who were loyal during the war. The bill's impact, however, turned out to be even more limited than it had initially appeared. Not only was the land that was made available swampy and of inferior quality, but few freedmen could afford to move long distances and then set themselves up with tools and supplies for a period of twelve months before the first crop was harvested and sold. Indeed, only about a thousand blacks were ultimately able to survive for five years and actually take possession under the act. Since there was also utter negligence in the implementation of the measure, it was evident that the Republicans saw the scheme as little more than a gesture, while the provision of land seemed clearly to be peripheral to the Republican majority's plans for the post-Emancipation South. Instead, the party's leaders focussed their energies on Lyman Trumbull's initiatives in the Senate.

The second of Trumbull's two proposals was a bill to define citizenship and civil rights as matters of federal, not just state, concern. While the purpose of the civil rights bill was to extend rights to blacks and, in the process, expand federal jurisdiction, the power of enforcement was limited to those instances in which states failed to provide protection for civil rights on their own. The bill's implementation rested therefore on "state action," not federal. And this was no oversight on Congress' part because Trumbull himself was quick to explain that the bill "will have no operation in any state where the laws are equal." Thus, the constitutional novelty of the measure was offset by a restriction that made it less effective than it had initially appeared.

Because these proposals were framed with circumspection, most Republican congressmen felt that they would receive the president's approval and thus form the basis for cooperation over southern policy. But an accommodation requires reciprocity, and Andrew Johnson chose not to seek common ground but to confront the bills' supporters. Lambasting Trumbull's measures because they involved an unwarranted expansion of federal power, he vetoed both of them. Then, in his messages accompanying the vetoes, he went out of his way to accentuate the differences between himself and Congress. He rejected conciliatory drafts submitted by his secretary of state, William H. Seward, in favor of an outright repudiation of Congress' authority to legislate for the southern states on the ground that, because they had not been readmitted, they were not represented. Since this was a non-negotiable position, Johnson evidently wanted, not a working relationship, but a fight. The Republicans responded by rallying their forces to try to repass both bills over the veto. Although they failed to muster two-thirds for the bureau bill, the civil rights law was enacted, the first time a major piece of legislation had been passed over a presidential veto.

The repercussions of the president's offensive were disastrous. From speeches he gave following his vetoes, it seems that he had intended to put distance between himself and the radical wing of the Republican party, but he had actually broken with the party's majority, which was desperately trying to heal the rift. While not excusable, Johnson's confusion about the alignment of forces within the Republican party is at least understandable, since historians have also been puzzled. Because the Republicans had immense majorities in Congress— they controlled the Senate by a margin of 42 to 11 and the House by 151 to 42—historians of the New South school concluded that the party was almost invincible. They believed that the Republicans were united and that, under the domination of the radicals, they were able to defy the president and pass whatever extreme legislation they wished. Consequently, these historians referred to the Republicans as simply "the Radicals" and to the party's southern policies as "Radical Reconstruction."

In recent years, however, there has been a major reevaluation of the Republican party and its policies. Revisionist historians have discovered, first, that the party was deeply divided over Reconstruction. Indeed, the issue was so complex and so divisive that it frequently threatened the party's survival. They have also found that the radicals, while vocal and assertive, never controlled the party or determined its legislation. Rather, they just seemed to be in the ascendant because of the role they played in the legislative process. In the major congressional debates on Reconstruction policy from 1866 to 1868, the radicals seized the initiative by proposing their own plan right at the start. This early dominance was misleading because, during the course of the debates on the Reconstruction measures, the radicals soon lost control. Their initial proposal was then either rejected or gutted, leaving them with the alternative of a rearguard struggle to keep as much as possible of their opening proposition. Invariably they lost, however, as the party's majority gave the legislation a tone and direction that was anathema to the radicals. This was the sequence when, for example, Congress produced its first Reconstruction plan in June 1866. Thaddeus Stevens, the leading radical in the House, complained afterwards that it "falls far short of my wishes." But he accepted the outcome, adding wistfully: "It is all that can be obtained in the present state of public affairs. . . . I will take all I can get in the cause of humanity and leave it to be perfected by better men in better times."

The disagreement was intense and it arose out of differing views about what had to be done with the South before it could be allowed readmission. The course of these intraparty debates can be followed by means of William R. Brock's *An American Crisis: Congress and Reconstruction, 1865–1867* (1963) and Michael Les Benedict's *A Compromise of Principle: Congressional Republicans and Reconstruction, 1863–1869*

(1974), which are respectively Revisionist and post-Revisionist in interpretative approach. To the party's radicals, the northern victory afforded a crucial opportunity in the country's history when the institutions and attitudes that had prevailed in the South under slavery could be changed. Readmission was therefore to be neither speedy nor superficial. Instead, the state governments established under Johnson's policy had to be dismantled and new men less attached to the old regime brought into positions of political power. While these changes were being made, radicals expected the South to be under military control and congressional supervision, its status resembling that of western territories prior to statehood or of conquered provinces after a foreign war.

A thoroughgoing reconstruction of the kind envisaged by the radicals would have involved other changes as well. Laws protecting the freedmen and establishing the foundations of a system of public education were frequently insisted upon. The vote for all black males was also demanded, while a few radicals regarded the confiscation of land from the rebels and its redistribution to the landless freedmen as a prerequisite. To Thaddeus Stevens, its main proponent, land was even more important than the vote as a means of guaranteeing the freedmen's independence and introducing change into the South. "Small independent landowners are the support and guardians of republican liberty" was how he once phrased his objective. The vote, by contrast, was vulnerable to manipulation by the freedmen's employers and would therefore, so Stevens felt, be no guarantee of political or economic independence.

There was, however, no precise agenda or blueprint that all radicals agreed upon. They did seem to be a more cohesive group and, in their approach to the problem, they shared certain assumptions that the rest of the party did not assent to. The moderates, as historians have tended to label the Republican majority, did not feel the need to start Reconstruction afresh or to prolong it. Instead, they wanted it settled as soon as possible, and all that was involved was the formulation of terms that the former Confederates had to accept before they could be readmitted. Among the conditions the moderates envisaged were a guarantee of legal protection to the freedmen; restrictions on the political influence of the ex-Confederates by disqualifying some of them from holding office; and, finally, provision for some degree of black voting, a stipulation that, by 1867, had broadened so as to include all adult males without qualification. Just like the radicals, the moderates differed among themselves about the relative importance of the specifics. Yet they agreed in their perception of Reconstruction as a set of terms to be proposed and negotiated rather than as a process of change to be imposed.

Within the organizational structure of the Republican party, the radicals and the moderates functioned, not as tightly organized units, but rather as loosely coordinated factions, with some shifting back and forth between them on particular issues. All the same, the existence of a serious division at a time when unity was so necessary does demand some explanation. In general, historians have offered two kinds of interpretation. The first claimed that a Republican congressman's stance on Reconstruction was determined by considerations that were primarily institutional. One suggestion was that a politician's radicalism was related to the size of his electoral margin. The more secure his seat the more extreme, and therefore radical, he could become. Alternatively, he might assume a radical stance in order to align himself with those within the party in his state who were opposed to his rival if the rival was a moderate. Plausible though it may seem, an institutional explanation excludes the possibility that those Republicans who became radicals did so out of conviction. Yet, of course, it is quite likely that this was the motivating factor. Indeed, some historians, in particular David Montgomery in his *Beyond Equality: Labor and the Radical Republicans, 1862–1872* (1967), have claimed that radicals were distinguished from moderates by their greater ideological and moral commitment. This argument is based on the observation that the radicals often came from areas of the North which were experiencing rapid economic growth and prosperity and which had been deeply affected by the religious revivalism of the antebellum years, with its emphasis on the autonomy and goodness of the individual. Imbued with a buoyant optimism about the nation and the individuals comprising it, the radicals saw Reconstruction as a great opportunity to introduce into the South those values and practices that seemed to be the source of so much human energy and material progress in their own region.

To this end, the privilege and caste that were so pervasive in the South were to be replaced by equality of opportunity and social mobility. Once free labor, universal education, and equal rights were implanted there, economic expansion and prosperity would soon follow. Perhaps the most sweeping depiction of the radicals' vision was offered by George W. Julian of Indiana. His version of a thoroughly reconstructed South called for the elimination of the region's "large estates, widely scattered settlements, wasteful agriculture, popular ignorance, social degradation, the decline of manufactures, contempt for honest labor, and a pampered oligarchy." After removing this blight, the Republicans would develop "small farms, thrifty tillage, free schools, social independence, flourishing manufactures and the arts, respect for honest labor, and equality of political rights." While other Republicans probably endorsed these general aspirations, the radicals pursued them with greater urgency and by means of sweeping proposals. As Charles Sumner, the Senate's leading radical, once said, "Where the abuse appears we must root it out. That is radicalism, I take it." In particular, they realized that, if these kinds of breakthroughs were to be achieved, the power of government had to be mobilized. So they were more utilitarian and activist in their plans for realizing these goals. In their view, the federal government was to be instrumental in reforming and reshaping the South; in extending the benefits of American citizenship and rights to all, regardless of race or origin; and in creating a unified, homogeneous nation out of a federation of disparate states.

Despite this emphasis on the role of ideas and beliefs in shaping radical policies, the radical Republicans were not just ideologues. Instead, they were working politicians who had to respond to partisan pressures as well as to be concerned about their own electoral prospects and political careers. Consequently, political imperatives like these would almost certainly have affected a congressman's vote on a particular question. Because of these considerations, the outcome of the debates over Reconstruction policy was rarely predictable. A more problematic consequence was that the peace terms that concluded the Civil War were not the product of calm deliberation behind closed doors but emerged instead out of a lengthy process of political wrangling and logrolling. Almost inevitably, therefore, they were a patchwork of propositions that too often lacked clarity and consistency. When they claimed executive primacy in Reconstruction policymaking, perhaps Presidents Lincoln and Johnson were aware of the pitfalls involved when the victor's postwar terms are formulated in public view by hundreds of legislators. Thus, it was not only unusual, if not unprecedented, for peace terms to be produced in this way, but it is quite possible that many of the problems besetting southern Reconstruction may have arisen because of the institutional context in which policy was formulated.

Despite the risk and the unorthodoxy, Congress was involved in determining Reconstruction policy for three entire years. During that time, it produced two different sets of final peace terms. They were the Fourteenth Amendment that was proposed in 1866 and the Military Reconstruction Act of March 1867, the latter requiring three further acts to clarify how it was to operate. Congress' initial plan was an amalgamation of a number of proposals considered by the Joint Committee on Reconstruction. Presented in the form of a constitutional amendment rather than a law, it consisted essentially of three sections dealing with what Congress believed to be the two fundamental elements in Reconstruction policy—the protection of the freedmen and the reduction of the leading Confederates' political power.

The proposed amendment defended southern blacks by reiterating, in its first clause, the legal and civil rights that had been set forth in the Civil Rights Act. An incentive for bestowing the right to vote on blacks was offered in the amendment's second clause which stipulated that a state's representation in Congress was to be based on the number of qualified voters, but with the restriction that, if individuals were excluded from voting on grounds other than for participation in the rebellion—that is, race—then a state's delegation would be reduced proportionately. Finally, the political power of the South's leadership was curbed by the requirement in the third clause that those who had held state or federal office before the war and then supported the rebellion were to be disqualified from holding office. To the radicals' mind, this was the only clause with any teeth in it, since the moderates in the House, led by John Bingham of New York, James Garfield of Ohio, and James Blaine of Maine, had already shot down the radicals' attempt to deny leading Southerners the vote on the grounds that it would result in a miniscule electorate and would also be unenforceable. But, to Thaddeus Stevens, exclusion of the ex-Confederates was essential. "Give us the third section or give us nothing" was his insistent demand during the debates.

While radicals like Stevens were prepared to accept the amendment for the sake of party unity, Andrew Johnson was not so cooperative. He sent Congress an angry message citing his objections and proceeded to make its proposal the issue in the upcoming congressional elections. Not only did he intend to defeat the congressional scheme but he also began to organize a political party to elect representatives committed to "My Policy," as he called it. To inaugurate this movement, he arranged a convention in Philadelphia in August to which delegates from both sections and both parties were invited. His aim was to revive the broad-gauged Union coalition of 1864 that had consisted of War Democrats as well as Republicans and had been the basis of the successful Lincoln-Johnson ticket. This time, however, he expected that the more radical Republicans would be unwilling to participate. Since the president also intended to exclude conspicuous secessionists from the South and antiwar Democrats, known as Copperheads, from the North, he must have been hoping that a bipartisan national coalition of the political center would rally around his policy. Headed by Republican moderates and a small group of pro-Johnson Republicans, it was to include most northern Democrats as well as those Southerners who had cooperated with the president's policy and shown themselves to be repentant.

What Johnson had in mind was a grand strategy for settling the question of southern readmission and, at the same time, realigning the political parties in the aftermath of the sectional crisis. Accordingly, he moved with determination to realize his vision of reorganizing the sectional Republican party so as to transform it into a party of National Union with support in both the North and the South. In this maneuver, the president was a force to be reckoned with. He employed his patronage power ruthlessly to purge opponents of his southern policy from federal office and, in a dramatic break with previous notions of presidential decorum, he campaigned across the northern states in what became known as the "Swing around the Circle." But all of his activity served only to convince each Republican officeholder that his own individual political future and that of his party was in grave danger, and so they all organized feverishly to defeat Johnson's National Union party candidates.

To this end, they were helped considerably by the outbreak of two ugly riots in the South during 1866, one in Memphis in early May and the other in New Orleans in July, both of which were, in essence, rampages by whites that resulted in the death of dozens of blacks. The two affrays were quite different in origin and character, however. The incident in Memphis took the form of a communal riot aimed at defending a predominantly Irish neighborhood against demobilized black soldiers from the nearby U.S. barracks and against black migrants moving into the city from the countryside. After days of violence and looting that spread into a neighboring black section, forty-seven blacks lay dead. By contrast, the New Orleans riot was fundamentally political in aim, since it was intended to prevent the reassembling of the state's constitutional convention of 1864. Incited by conservatives under the leadership of the mayor and the lieutenant governor, who feared that the convention would try to disfranchise former Confederates and thus regain control of the state for the declining Free State party, the city police and mobs of armed civilians simply attacked the Mechanics' Institute where the meeting of the conventionists was being held, killing thirty-seven delegates, all but three of whom were black, and wounding another two hundred. As in Memphis, it was nothing less than an unprovoked, cold-blooded massacre. The immediate impact of these outbreaks was to reveal the depth of racial violence and lawlessness prevailing in the South and thus to provide grim evidence for the northern electorate to conclude that the president's approach had been insufficiently firm. In the fall elections, therefore, voters resoundingly rejected Johnson's policy as well as his embryonic party.

Interestingly enough, despite his miscalculation over the differences between himself and the Republican majority, Johnson had recognized a problem that lay at the heart of the southern question, a problem that his opponents sometimes lost sight of. The Republicans could not afford to seat in Congress a southern delegation that would be likely to affiliate with the party's Democratic rivals. If that were to happen, the readmission of the South would jeopardize the hegemony, even the survival, of the party that had waged and won the war; and this naturally was unacceptable. By contrast, Johnson's conservative approach to Reconstruction would generate congressmen from the South who could not possibly align themselves with their enemies, the Republicans. As a result, he decided that his only course was to change the Republican party by making it national and conciliatory, so that the South's congressmen might then feel confident about joining it. The Republicans themselves, however, saw this move, not just as a threat but as a reversal of the priorities of Reconstruction. In their view, it was the South that had to change, not the Republicans. To this end, the region had to be politically reorganized so that the congressmen it selected were quite compatible with the northern Republicans. In other words, the South had to send Republicans to Congress.

Yet the disqualification clause in the proposed amendment, which was the only device the Republicans offered for achieving this essential aim, was insufficient. Without the creation of a new electorate based on the enfranchisement of the blacks, this prohibition alone would not have produced a congressional delegation composed of new elements from outside the region's political elite who represented different interests and values and who could therefore affiliate wholeheartedly with the Republicans. Nor incidentally would it have laid the foundations for a branch of the Republican party in the South, around which the political forces of Union and Reconstruction could organize and become established. This deficiency in the proposed amendment was very much on the minds of the Unionists of the South when they met in Philadelphia in September 1866 and they warned northern party leaders unavailingly of the likely dangers if no provision were made. Had the amendment constituted the final terms for southern readmission, its likely outcome was therefore that the Republicans' control of Congress would have been seriously threatened. That danger was, however, averted because, ironically, the South rejected the amendment.

Although Congress' plan offered the defeated Confederates the chance of readmission without having to submit either to black suffrage or to being represented by a delegation that did not share their priorities or represent their interests, they nevertheless refused overwhelmingly to ratify it. Only thirty-three votes in its favor were polled in all the southern state legislatures, with the exception of Tennessee. This apparently self-destructive reaction was not, however, uncalculated, as Michael Perman's *Reunion Without Compromise: The South and Reconstruction, 1865–1868* (1973) has shown. In fact, the South's political leaders believed they had no alternative but to reject it.

Risky though rejection was, there was thought to be a

known and greater danger in accepting the proffered terms. In the first place, the legislators who were being asked to ratify would be voluntarily endorsing their own removal from office because of the disqualification clause. Their second worry was that there was no guarantee that acceptance ensured southern readmission. Rather, by acceding to Congress' demands, they might be revealing their own weakness and opening themselves up to further exactions. This was even the opinion of Governor James L. Orr of South Carolina who was hardly an extremist. He warned that "the more palpably our submission to the laws and constitution of the United States and our acquiescence in the disastrous termination of the war is manifested the more exacting, tyrannical and humiliating to us become their demands." In other words, compliance was evidence of political weakness. Equally, it also indicated a lack of honor that invited the contempt of the North. It was one thing to accede to demands that were mandatory, but the proposed amendment was not binding at all. Consequently, as Jonathan Worth, Orr's counterpart in North Carolina, protested, "no generous man ought to expect us to hasten to the whipping post and invite the lash in advance of condemnation." The implied analogy of the willing slave was one that resonated deeply among white Southerners; Worth's use of it indicated the horror with which voluntary submission was regarded. "If we are to be degraded," the governor concluded, "we will retain some self-esteem by not making it self-abasement."

Besides the fears about acceptance, there was also the hope that rejection would be politically advantageous. After all, the defeat of the amendment would force the Republicans to devise an alternative. And there was a good chance that, in the process, internal disputes would arise that might deepen the existing divisions within the party and perhaps cause its breakup. Even if that did not occur, nonratification would buy time for the president, or the Supreme Court, or even the northern electorate, to demand that the harassment of the South be ended and an acceptable settlement worked out. Indeed, the Southerners already knew that the head of the executive branch was on their side, because Johnson had let it be known that he advised nonratification. Furthermore, they also had the support of the Democratic party, which had taken a public stance in favor of rejection. Meanwhile, the Supreme Court was giving Southerners encouragement with its decision in *ex parte Milligan* that military courts were unconstitutional in peacetime, thereby raising doubts about the possibility of a continuing military presence in the South.

Beset by all of these obstacles, the congressional Republicans had now to formulate another plan of Reconstruction. Yet there was great risk that the party's unity in Congress and its support in the northern electorate might be jeopardized if a policy were adopted that was more radical than the one the South had just rejected. Still, that was the only alternative open to them, unless they were prepared to yield to presidential pressure and southern recalcitrance. Since they were not about to reward southern defiance, they had to proceed toward tougher measures. And there were two possible options available to them. Either they could disperse the existing state governments that had been elected under the president's plan and then place the South under federal military supervision, with blacks enfranchised and all but the most loyal whites excluded from political power. Or Congress could press for a relatively speedy readmission of the South after it had complied with additional conditions, such as the granting of the suffrage to blacks and the ratification of the previously rejected amendment, with its provision for the exclusion from office of leading Confederates. In essence, these were the competing options proposed by the radicals and the moderates respectively.

The outcome of the intense debates in the brief lame-duck session of the Thirty-ninth Congress from January to March 1867 was a complicated piece of legislation which combined elements of both positions. The Reconstruction Act of March 1867 divided the South into five military districts, with the military possessing ultimate authority. At the same time, the Johnson governments were to continue in operation until the process of Reconstruction had been completed. During that time, blacks were to be registered to vote; leading Confederates were to be disfranchised and disqualified from holding office; new constitutions were to be framed and ratified that incorporated black suffrage; the pending Fourteenth Amendment was to be ratified, once a state legislature was chosen; and, finally, elections for state officials and congressional representatives were to be held. After that, the South would be readmitted to the Union and Reconstruction brought to completion.

Because the Reconstruction Act contained many features that were indisputably radical, historians have often concluded that the radical wing of the party got what it wanted and that it was therefore their measure. After all, Congress' new terms were mandatory, as the radicals had always insisted, since the South was not being asked to accept or reject them. In addition, the military was the ultimate authority in the Reconstruction process; it was superior to the existing civil governments and it was in charge of voter registration and elections. The radicalism of the law was also evident in its disregard of state rights, since it erased the political boundaries of states and overrode their authority. And, finally, of course, the act enfranchised thousands of blacks who, only a few years earlier, had been slaves. This last feature was a remarkable achievement that even Charles Sumner, the Senate's leading radical, acknowledged was "of greater value to Human Rights" than anything since Magna Carta. Despite all of this, the act was not the kind of measure the radical Republicans either wanted or thought wise.

Although it provided for military supervision and universal suffrage, the Reconstruction Act still lacked two elements that the radicals regarded as essential. Their first worry was that, even though curbed somewhat by the presence of the federal military, the state governments set up by Andrew Johnson in 1865 were to remain in operation throughout the entire process of political reorganization. The second problem was that the restrictions on the political power of the leading ex-Confederates were quite inadequate. Indeed, until the very last day before the bill was finally passed, there were no curbs on them except the third clause of the pending amendment preventing many of them from holding office. Even then, this check would not go into effect until the amendment was ratified at the end of the Reconstruction process. This shortsightedness worried the radicals a great deal, and they warned of the dire consequences if the bill were passed in that limited form. Insisting that there should be "greater safeguards than any that are supplied in this very hasty and crude act of legislation," Sumner feared that, although the slaves were now voting, "their masters are left in power to domineer, and even to organize." "It is horribly defective," he concluded regretfully. Thomas Williams of Pennsylvania, a radical in the House, went so far as to urge no action at all. "I want evidence that the hearts of their people are changed. . . . We can govern them outside of the Union; we cannot govern them inside of it, with the alliances they will form here [in Congress]." But no one was more grim about the implications of the proposed legislation than Williams's colleague from Pennsylvania, Thaddeus Stevens. In his view, the bill's import was quite clear. Congress was simply "hugging and caressing those whose hands are red and whose garments are dripping with the blood of our and their murdered kindred."

By contrast with the radicals' scorn, the moderate Republicans regarded the proposal with some pride. Senator William Stewart of Nevada described it as "a grand measure of justice and generosity." Similarly, John Sherman of Ohio, the famous general's brother, who had steered the bill through the Senate, was gratified that, because no Southerners had been denied the right to vote, the new governments to be created in the South would be based "upon the permanent foundation of universal liberty and universal equality and would stand upon the consent of the governed, white and black, former slaves and former masters." For the moderates, the virtue of the bill in its current form was that it provided a formula for Reconstruction that would restore the South to the Union promptly while ensuring that no one was prevented from exercising their right to vote. Universal suffrage was, therefore, a means for creating a loyal constituency in the South that was inclusive and, so the moderates believed, just. For the radicals, however, those very same qualities were the bill's weakness. They wanted reconstruction to take time and be thorough, and they wanted the military to be in charge and the rebels kept out. Because the proposed scheme for southern reconstruction amounted to little more than a mechanism for the immediate readmission of the region to Congress, rather than for its government prior to readmission, it fell "far short," according to Charles Sumner, "of what a patriotic Congress ought to supply for the safety of the Republic."

At the eleventh hour during the night of 19 February, just before the final votes on the bill the next day, the radicals in the House managed to rush through two significant amendments to strengthen the proposal. The first declared the existing Johnson governments in the South to be "provisional only" and subject to the military's interference if necessary. The second extended the Confederate disqualification from office so as to include disfranchisement as well. By means of this last-minute maneuver—which the Democrats supported in the hope of defeating the bill because its provisions were too extreme for the moderates to approve—the radicals had put some teeth into the measure. But its basic assumptions they still opposed. Despite these additions, which in fact were included in the final act, Sumner still complained soon after its passage that "It has presented no complete system, and it has provided no machinery for reconstruction." At this point, the moderates were also dissatisfied. John Sherman announced that "these amendments are not the amendments of the Union party," a majority of which had only a day or so earlier offered "a proposition which contained no prohibition of any man from exercising the elective franchise." Another nonradical, Senator John B. Henderson of Missouri, was also reluctant to support the measure as amended, but he decided nonetheless to concur because "It has the assent of my party friends, who think, perhaps, that it is better than nothing." In its essentials, however, the bill still belonged to the moderates. But now even they were dissatisfied with its provisions.

This anxious three-week session of the expiring Thirty-ninth Congress had produced a law that laid down the final terms for reconstructing the South. Yet it had been drawn up in great haste and was ultimately to generate little enthusiasm from either faction. Undeniably significant though the settlement was, Senator Timothy Howe of Wisconsin had nevertheless to admit that "Alas! there was nothing grand about it. Congress has never seemed . . . more querulous, distracted, incoherent and ignoble."

Although disappointed about the outcome, Congress could not even relax its guard once the law was passed. As expected, it soon received a resounding veto from Andrew Johnson. Because of this, Congress' hope that its responsibility for Reconstruction would end when it produced a set of final terms was unfortunately not about to be satisfied. Instead, the struggle resumed with unabated intensity. First, the Republicans had to round up enough votes to secure a two-thirds majority, a task that was not so easily accomplished. In addition, the process of political reorganization laid down by the act was so complex that it continued to preoccupy Congress and even required further legislation to clarify the intent of the initial law.

These difficulties were aggravated by the unceasing efforts on the part of the president to thwart the implementation of the act. He proceeded to remove military commanders who, in his view, were interpreting the Reconstruction Act too liberally. He also challenged the authority of the law when, in May 1867, he required Attorney General Henry Stanbery to present an official opinion concerning both the extent of the military's jurisdiction and the qualifications for voter registration in the South. He even tried, during the winter of 1867–68, to remove Secretary of War Edwin Stanton because he was too sympathetic to Congress' aims. And, finally, he attempted to control General Ulysses S. Grant who, as general-in-chief, was at the head of the military command structure and there-

fore possessed considerable influence over southern operations. As a result, Congress had to pass three more Reconstruction Acts to protect and clarify the original one.

Johnson's obstruction was so relentless and its impact on
the course of events in the South so disruptive that the Republicans began to think that his removal, or at least immo-
bilization, was essential to save Reconstruction from being
fatally undermined. Accordingly, talk about impeachment,
which had surfaced earlier during 1866, began to assume con-
crete form. During the winter of 1867, a move to impeach the
president was formally introduced. This drive failed, but it
was revived a few months later when, in February 1868, Johnson literally forced Stanton out of his office. In failing to obtain
the consent of the Senate, he had quite probably acted in vi-
olation of the Tenure of Office Act, which Congress had passed
a year earlier for the precise purpose of protecting Congress'
supporters in the cabinet, Stanton in particular. This was
thought to provide sufficient grounds for action, since impeachment was a legal matter and Johnson had just committed
an indictable offense by breaking the law.

The issues involved were, of course, actually far greater.
For this reason, the impeachment trial itself has usually been
viewed as a rather petty and tawdry procedure that served to
obscure deeper purposes. Johnson's defenders have seen the
attempt to remove the president as the culmination of a plot
by Republican politicians to eliminate the major obstacle in
the way of their desire to dominate the South. Tied to this
ambition, it was thought, was a long-range plan to achieve the
supremacy of the legislative over the executive and judicial
branches of the federal government, and the impeachment of
the president was believed to be central to the Republicans'
purpose. More recently, however, historians have come to see
Johnson, not as an embattled president trying to defend the
South and the constitution from the assaults of the unbridled Republican majority in Congress, but as an embittered
and obstinate politician determined to obstruct the will of Congress in its struggle to reconstruct the South. Even so, Eric

McKitrick, who was one of those who took this view, still felt compelled to denigrate the Johnson impeachment, calling it "a great act of ill-directed passion" and little more than "a long-needed psychological blow-off."

The tension and acerbity that permeated the impeachment proceedings arose out of the dilemma in which the Republicans found themselves. Impeachment appeared to be a highly risky step but one which nevertheless was politically necessary. Failure to convict Johnson was not only quite possible but, if that were actually to be the outcome, it would damage the party seriously. Yet a refusal even to attempt impeachment would have left him free to interfere in the South at a critical juncture when the already-embattled southern Republicans were trying to get their new state constitutions ratified. Indeed, congressmen were being besieged with warnings from the South that another presidential onslaught might be disastrous. Also involved in impeachment was a last-ditch attempt by the radicals to obtain influence in their party, since they hoped to replace Johnson with one of their own, Benjamin F. Wade, the president *pro tem* of the Senate. Once installed in the White House, Wade would have a good chance of securing the Republican presidential nomination later that year.

Whatever long-term aims the impeachers, or at least some of them, may have had in mind went unrealized because the Senate voted, by a narrow margin and with the help of seven Republicans, against conviction. In the short run, the trial kept the president preoccupied for several months and enabled the Republicans to carry out their task of Reconstruction. Meanwhile, they convinced Ulysses Grant, who had broken with Johnson in late 1867, to accept their party's nomination for president in 1868. Sustained by the general's popularity and by the party's successful reorganization and readmission of all but three of the former Confederate states by June 1868, the Republicans were able to carry the election decisively. They won every state except Oregon, New Jersey, and New York in the North; Delaware, Kentucky, and Maryland in the Border states; and Louisiana and Georgia in the South. With Grant's political victory, the peace that his military triumph had won earlier was at last secured. But it had taken three perilous and exhausting years to accomplish. Even then, Grant's campaign pledge, "Let Us Have Peace," would prove to be little more than a pious hope.

The Southern Republicans

With the return of the South to Congress in June 1868, Reconstruction was nominally completed. Although the term "reconstruction" is customarily used to describe the entire period from 1865 to 1877, the Reconstruction Acts themselves dealt only with the requirements for readmission and the procedure for forming and electing new governments in the South. Since federal relations had been restored and the southern states were now governing themselves, the mandate of the acts had essentially been fulfilled. But the outcome of Reconstruction would not be decided until these newly established Republican administrations had demonstrated their ability, not merely to survive, but to govern and bring about changes in southern life. Reconstruction was not over therefore; rather, it was just beginning.

This dilemma was to prove the major stumbling block in sustaining Reconstruction in the South and bringing it to a successful conclusion. Most Republican congressmen who had framed the Reconstruction Acts, and then spent a year of intense activity and acute anxiety implementing them, considered the task of Reconstruction to be finished by 1868. Indeed, they had resisted radical pressures for an open-ended, long-term process of Reconstruction for the simple reason that they wanted the matter settled expeditiously, thereby removing the uncertainty and instability. Because further involvement was what they had been at pains to avoid, the Republican majority had conceived of Reconstruction in limited terms. They had rejected military rule and the confiscation and redistribution of land, thereby excluding the possibility of significant change. Instead, they had opted for a political solution to the problem of Reconstruction. Even then, the political reorganization that the congressional Republicans had in mind was construed narrowly, since the former Confederates and the opponents of Reconstruction were not banned from political activity altogether but could form a party of opposition to counter the fledgling Republicans and their black supporters. Reconstruction was conceived therefore as a political question, and it was to function within the context of a conventional electoral system with competing political parties, just like those in the states outside the South.

Understandable though this choice may have been, it was to prove impractical and virtually self-defeating. In the first place, the means employed to sustain Reconstruction were not the limited, conservative ones that their proponents had intended. Although military rule had been rejected, the military had administered the whole process of voter registration and constitutional revision that had been involved in reconstructing the South during 1867 and 1868. Futhermore, the participation of thousands of blacks in southern politics may have been seen by the moderates as less radical than extended military occupation but, to southern whites, it was an outrage not easily tolerated. Consequently, black voting gave the Republicans as well as Reconstruction itself an aura of radicalism, even illegitimacy, right from the start. Thus, the means for accomplishing the limited and rapid Reconstruction that was intended were proving to be more radical and provocative perhaps than the end itself.

The second difficulty generated by the kind of plan espoused by Congress was that it required constant involvement by the federal government rather than providing the mechanism for withdrawal that had been hoped for. The political structure that had been created in the South was simply too restricted in scope and power to be able to sustain itself adequately. So it needed continual reinforcement to prop it up. Troops were needed to protect the vulnerable Republican governments or to put down violence against their supporters. Meanwhile, congressional action was constantly required to monitor southern elections and protect black voting rights. As a result, the more the federal authorities involved themselves in southern politics after 1868, the more they acknowledged the inadequacy of their original plan and, in fact, departed from their initial assumptions and goals. Enforcing Reconstruction, therefore, not only kept it alive as a perplexing and troublesome problem, but also raised new issues about, for example, federal-state relations and the role of the military in civil matters.

Reconstruction lasted for as long as the Republican party stayed in power, and its ability to do so varied from state to state. Those that remained Republican the longest were Louisiana, South Carolina, and Florida, where the party lost control early in 1877 as a result of the concession Rutherford Hayes made to obtain the presidency. The previous year, Mississippi fell to the Democrats, while Arkansas and Alabama were lost in 1874 and Texas in 1873. As early as 1870, the Republicans were defeated in Georgia. That same year, they had lost control of the legislative branch in North Carolina and, by 1875, the whole state was Democratic. Meanwhile, Virginia virtually avoided Reconstruction because the Republicans never gained exclusive control over the state, since they initially shared power with the Democrats and then lost it altogether in 1873.

The Republican party therefore held effective power in the South for only a brief time, virtually six years from 1868 until about 1874. The difficulties it experienced cannot, however, be attributed solely to the existence of a relentlessly hostile Democratic opposition, or to other forces external to it. Within the party itself, there were immense problems. Essentially, they revolved around the question of what kind of party it was to be and what role it was to play in southern politics. This was not easy to decide because, from the very beginning, southern Republicanism was a coalition of conflicting elements. This Republican coalition was a microcosm of the regional and racial antagonisms generated by the crisis of the Civil War and Reconstruction. Its membership consisted of

Northerners and Southerners as well as blacks and whites, who fell into three categories, known pejoratively as "carpetbaggers," "scalawags," and "Negroes." Because they were, for the most part, a cadre of new political leaders and activists and because they took considerable risk in attaching themselves to a party that had been introduced forcibly into the former Confederacy, historians have been greatly intrigued about these men and have wanted to discover who they were and why they joined the Republicans. More recently, they have also begun to examine the role and relative influence of each group within the party.

The "carpetbaggers" were white Northerners who were in the South after the war, either because they saw the region as a new frontier of economic and political opportunity or because they felt a humanitarian responsibility to participate in religious and educational work among the former slaves. Many of them, however, did not have to travel to the South once the war was over because they were already there as workers among the freedmen, as federal officials, or as Union soldiers. For example, Harrison Reed who was to become Florida's first Republican governor in 1868 had left Wisconsin and gone south during the war, first as a treasury agent and then as a post office official. He was a central figure in the formation of the state's Republican party in 1867 and then took the lead in steering it in a conservative direction and focussing its attention on developing the state's material resources, particularly its railroads. Albert Morgan was also from Wisconsin and had similar motives of personal advancement when he decided to stay in Mississippi after his demobilization from the U.S. army. He and his brother initially bought a plantation. When they failed at that as well as at running a sawmill, he reckoned that Republican politics offered an alternative livelihood. Once involved, however, Morgan became an active member of the party's radical wing who struggled and risked his life to keep the besieged organization afloat in the Delta county of Yazoo. Also involved in Mississippi Republicanism was Adelbert Ames. A well-connected New Englander, Ames had had a remarkably distinguished war record, receiving the Congressional Medal of Honor and rising to brigadier general before the age of thirty. After the war, he decided that he would devote himself to the work of Reconstruction by staying in the South. He first headed the Freedmen's Bureau in Mississippi and then became a pivotal force in Republican politics there as the leader of the party's radical faction. By 1870, he was a U.S. senator and, after 1874, governor.

Whatever their motives and circumstances, Northerners almost invariably associated with the Republicans, and it was this activity that provoked the derisive epithet of "carpetbagger." As William M. Lowe, a Democratic congressman from north Alabama, told a congressional committee investigating the Klan in 1871, "the term 'carpetbagger' was applied to the office-seeker from the North who came here seeking office by the negroes, by arraying their political passions and prejudices against the white people of the community." Naturally, he added, these were "men of bad character." By contrast, those Northerners who confined their activities to economic pursuits, such as planting and trade, and stayed away from sympathetic involvement with the freedmen and from Republican politics, were rarely castigated as carpetbaggers.

Since the fledgling party was northern in origin and was intended to spread northern values into the South, it naturally welcomed northern men into its ranks. Moreover, because it needed contacts and leverage in the North, those who were given positions in the new party had either had some previous political experience there or were Northerners working for the federal treasury or customs departments. Finally, of course, the Republicans' large and politically inexperienced black electorate offered a constituency for northern aspirants for office who naturally had no prior support in the region. From the outset, therefore, newcomers became influential in the party, not as a voting bloc since their numbers were so few, but as officeholders and legislators.

In 1867–1869, when the Republican party was first establishing itself in the South, Northerners were the most active and formative element. This was particularly evident in the conventions that were assembled in 1867 under the Reconstruction Acts to rewrite the constitutions of the southern states. Although they comprised just under 16 percent of the membership of the conventions, newcomers nevertheless chaired over half of the most important committees which framed the bills of rights and the articles on education and the suffrage. Since they were from the North, they were also thought to be better qualified to serve in Congress, so that, initially, carpetbaggers were well-represented in the first Republican delegations elected in 1868 and 1869. Their incidence diminished as time passed, except in Louisiana, Mississippi, South Carolina, and Florida. It seems that, in states like these where the party's electoral base was relatively secure, it selected newcomers, or sometimes blacks, for Congress; but when it was weak and needed to get white support, it chose native Southerners instead.

Because newcomers relied so heavily on blacks as their constituency, they were most likely to be prominent and numerous in those states that had sizable black electorates and, consequently, the strongest Republican parties. Furthermore, since blacks were their constituents, Northerners identified with their need for civil rights, education, physical protection from white violence, and social services, all of which required increased government expenditures and taxation. Thus, they were usually associated with the more radical wing of the party. Many of the Northerners were also eager to develop their state's economic resources through railroad building and manufacturing, though they had to be careful not to do so at the expense of those other issues that were of especial concern to blacks. The political cost of reversing these priorities could be serious, as several carpetbaggers, like Governors Powell Clayton of Arkansas, Henry C. Warmoth of Louisiana, and Harrison Reed of Florida soon discovered. For their black support simply evaporated once it was clear what their policy preferences were.

Another basis for northern influence was their control of the federal patronage since, as might be expected, Northerners were invariably the U.S. customs collectors and revenue agents in the South. In a party with few resources and hosts of impecunious applicants for positions, the newcomers' access to federal jobs gave them considerable leverage for consolidating their own influence and rewarding their friends. In fact, controlling patronage and retaining office invariably became an end in itself for the carpetbaggers, because it was an essential means of support for men who were uprooted and lacked social acceptance and alternative sources of income. Their opponents at the time as well as the New South historians later both accused the Northerners of going into politics solely for the spoils. Although they made this insinuation to denigrate the despised carpetbaggers, it is clear that, no matter how idealistic many were in deciding to cast their lot with the Republicans, the pressure of their circumstances forced them to hang on to office for the income and security it provided.

The second component of the new party also needed the remuneration and status of office, but rarely obtained it. Blacks generated the overwhelming majority of the party's votes yet, because the white leaders wanted it for themselves and because blacks feared the consequences of identifying the party too closely with their race, the influence of the latter was kept to a minimum. But, in time—especially in those states like South Carolina, Mississippi, and Louisiana where blacks were a majority of the electorate—they were able to organize and obtain greater representation as legislators and executive officials. In Mississippi, for example, pressure from the blacks forced the party to nominate one of their number for lieutenant governor in 1875, while South Carolina's black Republicans, under the leadership of Congressman Robert B. Elliott, were virtually in charge of the party apparatus by 1874 and had extensive influence in the assembly through their control of important committee chairmanships.

The presence of numerous blacks in public offices to which they had been elected or appointed by the Republicans was one of the most remarkable features of Reconstruction. Sixteen blacks went to Congress during the period, two of whom were senators, both from Mississippi. More than half of the congressmen came from South Carolina and Alabama, eight and three respectively, while North Carolina, Georgia, Florida, and even Louisiana and Mississippi, sent only one each. But none came from Texas and Arkansas because those states were dominated by native whites and Northerners, respectively. Although no black was elected governor, several served as secretary of state, lieutenant governor, and superintendent of public instruction, and one, Jonathan Wright, sat on the supreme court of South Carolina from 1871 to 1877. Nevertheless, these few blacks in major offices amounted to a far from adequate representation for a group that provided the Republican party with the bulk of its electoral support. This pattern continued at the local level where blacks held office only rarely. Even in South Carolina, where there was a considerable black elite to draw from, only a handful served in county government as sheriff, auditor, treasurer, probate judge, and clerk of the court. Black officeholders were therefore hardly as ubiquitous as the New South historians, with their claims of "Africanization" and "Black Reconstruction," had charged.

At the same time, it would be quite erroneous to underestimate the quality and contribution of those blacks who attained positions of leadership during Reconstruction. As a group, they were, it is true, politically inexperienced. But a majority was educated and had achieved prominence in black society through activity in the Freedmen's Bureau, the missionary schools, or black religious and civic organizations. Often, too, they had been relatively successful as artisans, farmers, professionals, or small businessmen. Naturally enough, most officeholding blacks had been free before the war and frequently, as was the case particularly in New Orleans and Charleston, they were mulattoes who enjoyed a privileged economic and social status because of the sponsorship of their white fathers. This profile of black political leadership has emerged in recent years as a result of numerous studies aimed at discovering the details of the lives of these little-known but highly significant figures. Biographies of black congressmen such as Robert Smalls and Robert B. Elliott of South Carolina, James Rapier of Alabama, and Josiah Walls of Florida have appeared, as have group studies of black politicians in South Carolina, Louisiana, and Georgia. This greater knowledge of their careers has produced a reassessment of their abilities and a reversal of the earlier view that dismissed them as essentially unqualified and corrupt.

Historians are now going beyond the rehabilitation of their reputations to examine how black politicians functioned within the Republican coalition. This emphasis on the way they used office, rather than just their qualifications for holding it, has resulted in several important insights. The first is that blacks were politically skillful, and they maneuvered with some degree of success to develop influence. After initially playing second fiddle to the more experienced whites, they decided to mobilize their forces and demand that blacks be nominated for positions inside the party apparatus and that they be given an increased share of appointive offices as well as jobs in public services such as the police and fire departments and the educational system. Meanwhile, they organized effectively to get blacks on the Republican ticket in districts with black majorities. Finally, they expanded their influence in several state legislatures by seizing key committee assignments, a strategy that was particularly successful in South Carolina and Mississippi by the early 1870s.

A second feature of the black leadership was that, despite its general cohesiveness, it was sometimes troubled with friction. Most often, dissension arose when blacks were courted by competing white factions within the party. This occurred frequently in Alabama and Florida during the 1870s. In South Carolina, blacks divided in 1875–76 when Governor Daniel Chamberlain embarked on a risky maneuver to form an alliance with the more conciliatory wing of the Democratic party. From time to time, division also arose because disagreements emerged among blacks themselves. For instance, in Louisiana from 1869 to 1871, political rivalry between Oscar Dunn and P. B. S. Pinchback caused a serious rift among black Republicans. Also evident, to some extent, was a division based on social status and economic interest. Particularly in Charleston and New Orleans, there was a substantial Negro elite that was propertied, free-born and usually mulatto. Recently, several historians, chiefly Thomas Holt in his study of black political leaders in South Carolina, entitled *Black Over White* (1977), have claimed that they acted self-consciously to preserve their privileged position. To this end, they voted for a literary and property qualification on the suffrage and they sometimes opposed legislation to protect agricultural laborers against their employers. This split between the free-born browns and the black former slaves was probably most evident in Charleston where many browns went so far as to support Chamberlain's break with the party's black electoral base. Elsewhere, however, the rift between browns and blacks was of limited political significance because the former were either too few numerically to be of consequence or else they were aware that, as was the case in New Orleans, their own prospects and those of the mass of freedmen were interdependent.

The third facet of Negro politics that has recently become more evident was the constant need to form working relationships with white Republican politicians and voters. Even though a black politician could not be elected without a black electoral base, he also could not succeed without cooperation from whites. Those like Aaron A. Bradley and Tunis Campbell in Georgia who purposefully spurned white support soon became marginal. Thus, the success of a black politician depended upon his skill in consolidating his black constituency while simultaneously developing essential backing from whites, both within his district and inside the party organization. But interracial coalitions and alliances were difficult to put together and even more difficult to sustain. After all, white voters were reluctant to support black candidates, while the Northerners who were the more likely white allies of black politicians were concurrently competing with them to represent the same black constituency.

The last, and the pivotal, element in the Republican coalition was the native whites, or "scalawags" as they have been labeled by their detractors. The scalawags were critical because the growth and continuation of southern Republicanism depended upon its ability to gain support from the resident population. In every state, except possibly South Carolina, Mississippi, and Louisiana, Republicans had to be able to attract substantial numbers of white votes in order to win elections and remain viable. Paradoxically, however, success in this attempt would be a mixed blessing because it would precipitate another vexing problem. If the support of native whites was secured and on the increase, the influence of the scalawags within the party was likely to grow proportionately. This expansion would inevitably occur at the expense of the Northerners, who had no natural southern constituency, as well as of the blacks, whose loyalty to the party was assumed and who therefore did not need courting. Thus, the search for white votes, so necessary for the party's survival, was ironically the catalyst for a power struggle that threatened its harmony, and perhaps ultimately its existence.

Nevertheless, the attempt had to be made because this potential support, if not won over by the Republicans, would be secured by their Democratic rivals. Indeed, the Democrats lost no time in trying to stop native whites from defecting to the Republicans by stigmatizing them as "unprincipled office-seekers" and "traitors" to their race and section. While these epithets may have convinced historians of the New South school about the character of the scalawags and their motives for joining the Republicans, they are clearly inadequate as explanations of a change of allegiance fraught with personal risk and political significance. Several alternative interpretations of who the native Republicans were and why they affiliated with the party have been proposed by historians in recent years. One suggests that, like Governor James L. Alcorn of Mississippi or Provisional Governor Lewis Parsons of Alabama, they were former Whigs who, having been politically unattached since the mid-1850s, naturally gravitated to a new party that was opposed to their bitter rivals, the Democrats.

Usually, these Whigs were influential politicians who had tried to counter the region's precipitous endorsement of disunion in the crisis of 1860–61, or they were men of economic means, probably merchants or manufacturers, who were attracted by the Whigs' national and more activist economic policies. By contrast, another view argued that native Republicans were more likely to be former Democrats than ex-Whigs. Moreover, they were probably small farmers from the uplands where there had been considerable wartime opposition to the Confederacy as well as to the economic and political power of the black belt and the towns. Yet a third approach—in some ways similar to the second—asserted that those native whites who joined the Republican party did so because they were political dissenters who had opposed the established leadership before as well as during the war; typical were politicians like Senator John Pool and Governor William W. Holden of North Carolina. In this contest, they had fought to democratize state politics and government and had resisted secession and sought a negotiated peace. Because these dissenters saw Republicanism as a sympathetic force in that it was composed of outsiders and committed to reform, they threw in their lot with it. Thus, it was not their class position or past party allegiance but rather their ideology and stance on political issues that determined their affiliation with the Republicans.

Although this disagreement seems to indicate that historians are hopelessly at odds about the identity of the scalawags, it actually reveals the diversity of the native white Republicans themselves. In effect, each interpretation simply highlights a particular facet or strand in the group's composition. For the Republican party, in fact, appealed to a number of different elements in southern political life. Unfortunately, however, these groups and their aspirations were rarely compatible. So a choice had to be made as to which kind of support the party wanted to attract and, therefore, what kind of party it wanted to become. Was the Republican party in the South to be a party of protest appealing to the disadvantaged and excluded? Or was it to be a more traditional political party seeking acceptance and acquiring respectability through its capacity to reassure men of wealth and position and attract politicians with established reputations?

The choice about the kind of support the Republicans would seek out was determined, to a large extent, by the scalawags themselves. Those that joined the party in its formative years and held office under it were, in general, men who had previously been active in southern politics. Although only a few had been as prominent as the former governor of Georgia, Joseph E. Brown, or Congressman Alexander White of Alabama, most of them affiliated with the Republicans in the hope of continuing their political careers and acting as a moderating influence on the party's future direction. Thus, the native white leadership was a force of conservatism seeking to "southernize" the party, not radicalize it. Indeed, in states such as Texas, North Carolina, and Georgia where natives dominated the Republicans, the party was at its most cautious and accommodating, while elsewhere, in Mississippi and Alabama, for example, the native faction was invariably more conciliatory than its northern and black rival.

The result was that the Republicans, whose future depended upon their ability to develop a following among the local whites, found themselves appealing to established interests and influential individuals and trying to win their respect. This meant that they took for granted the contribution and the needs of the black population and overlooked the possibility of attracting disadvantaged and disaffected whites. This choice was probably unavoidable for a newly formed political party whose right to exist was being challenged and whose survival in a competitive electoral system required that it appeal successfully to a majority of the voters. The impact of this preference on the Republican party itself was, however, to plunge it into a state of constant tension between what the party actually was and what it wanted to become. The Republicans' identity was therefore ambiguous and its appeal to native whites lacked both force and focus.

The Achievement of Southern Reconstruction

Under the Reconstruction Act, the southern states were required to write new constitutions before they could be readmitted to Congress. As a result, conventions met in nine states during the winter of 1867–68 (Texas, because of its size and sparse population, was delayed until 1869). The constitutions they produced established the political perimeters and governmental framework of the new order ushered in by Reconstruction. Because these were the first political assemblages elected since blacks were enfranchised, they would therefore reveal how extensive were the changes resulting from this dramatic breakthrough. One innovation was apparent at the outset, since there were 258 blacks among the 1,027 convention delegates. All the same, none of the constitutions that these Republican-dominated conventions created was sweepingly radical, though they were undoubtedly innovative as well as progressive.

The changes they introduced were intended, first, to reduce privilege and increase participation and, second, to expand the role of government in providing services. On the first count, the constitutions lowered or removed age and property qualifications for holding office and made most positions elective rather than appointive. Also, they frequently reduced the overrepresentation of the plantation counties. The other kind of change made government responsible for creating institutions to care for orphans, the insane, and the deaf and dumb. In addition, penitentiaries were to be built and staffed and a system of public education established. This governmental activism was then facilitated by granting increased power to the executive branch. Finally, several state governments provided relief to those who were suffering economically by staying the payment of debts and, on occasion, exempting homesteads from seizure by creditors.

These reforms were essentially liberal and democratic in nature. When the conventions considered the possibility of more extensive changes, they invariably backed off. One of these was the critical question of making land available to the landless, in particular the freedmen. Although land confiscation was discussed in every convention, it was never seriously entertained. Two states, Louisiana and South Carolina, decided to petition Congress to provide federal funds for the purchase of plantations which were then to be subdivided and sold at low prices. Nothing came of these requests for federal action, while only one state, South Carolina, did anything on its own. This took the form of a land commission that was provided with funds consisting of state securities which it was to use to buy up plantations. The land that was obtained in this way was then to be sold cheaply to settlers, regardless of race. The commission's impact was, however, only marginal, since it was never given much attention by the Republican-controlled state government and was often mismanaged. In its twenty-year existence, it bought 112,000 acres and aided about 14,000 families, who were almost exclusively black. But neither the value and amount of land nor the beneficiaries were great enough to be of consequence. The commission may well have been the last gasp of the movement for post-Emancipation land reform.

Indeed, because of other actions the conventions took, it became more difficult, not less, for land to change hands. This was the effect of the relief measures aimed at protecting distressed farmers who were being pursued by their creditors. The stay laws and homestead exemption provisions simply enabled debtors, many of whom were planters rather than impoverished small farmers, to hold on to their homes and farms. This, in turn, kept their property off the market where others, mainly the landless, might have had a chance to buy. Thus, debtor relief ironically destroyed whatever opportunities remained for land reform and redistribution.

/ Another opportunity was lost by the conventions' approach to the question of integrated education. Unlike land reform, this issue was debated extensively. The creation of a system of public education offered the chance to break down patterns of prejudice and establish racial equality by means of mixed schooling. Yet, in fact, only Louisiana required that black and white children attend the same schools. Elsewhere, the conventions avoided the question of racial mixing by asserting simply that children be admitted regardless of race. This fear of making mixed schools mandatory was often shared by blacks themselves, because they worried that public education in general might be jeopardized if integration were required and, in response, whites withdrew their children. Indeed, this worry was not unrealistic, since that is exactly what happened in Louisiana with the exception of a small district in New Orleans. Black reluctance about mixing also arose out of a concern that their children's autonomy and self-esteem might be undermined by having to conform, so soon after slavery, to white norms imposed by white teachers. As Francis Cardozo, who was the black chairperson of the education committee in South Carolina's convention, had noted: "I have no doubt, in most localities, colored people would prefer separate schools, particularly until some of the present prejudice against their race is removed." There was an opposing perspective on the issue that was articulated by Benjamin F. Randolph, another black Republican from South Carolina whose promising political career was soon to be ended by assassination. He warned against uncomplaining resignation, arguing instead: "We are laying the foundation of a new structure here, and the time has come when we shall have to meet things squarely." Under the circumstances, however, Randolph's preference turned out to be unobtainable; so separate schooling was accepted.

A third indicator of the conventions' caution was their decision about whether to allow leading rebels to vote. Disfranchisement had already been resorted to in the Reconstruction Act. Now, its extension to the state level was often thought necessary in view of the narrowness of the Republicans' electoral base in the South. Until the party became established, the proscription of former Confederates who were almost certain to be political opponents was believed, especially by the party's radicals, to be indispensable. But others argued that excluding political opponents and withholding the suffrage was unwise when the Republicans needed to win the respect of whites and secure the unrestricted right to vote for blacks. The upshot was that most states did not impose political disabilities in their constitutions, while those that did soon removed them. In fact, the Virginia and Mississippi constitutions were initially rejected by the voters, primarily because they disfranchised leading Confederates. Congress responded to this setback by requiring that the documents be resubmitted, with the disabling clause voted on separately. When this was done, it was defeated each time. A year later, in 1870, the Republican governors of Alabama and Louisiana recommended that disfranchisement be ended, and both legislatures complied. Thereafter, only Arkansas restricted Confederate voting. The significance of this development was that, by surrendering what was a problematic, yet crucial, device for curbing their opponents' vote, the Republicans had left themselves no electoral alternative other than to pursue unequivocally a political strategy aimed at winning over white support. By this time, radicals like Morgan Hamilton of Texas were convinced that the party had "recruited too many already, and the more it takes in the worse for the cause of Republicanism." Indeed, the party was "hopelessly broken-down," so Senator Hamilton thought, because its survival now depended almost entirely upon its ability to attract southern whites.

The constitutional settlement of 1868–69 provided the framework within which the newly elected Republican administrations would have to operate. But this was not the only context that party leaders had to consider. Catapulted into power before it had had time to establish its credentials and build a following, the party was now further constrained by the need to administer and govern. As a result, the governments' own legitimacy and their ability to gain respect became a matter of primary concern. The question therefore arose as to whether recognition should be sought at the expense of reforms that were quite likely to prove unsettling and a threat to established interests. The extent to which the Republicans were caught in this dilemma of being a party of reform and change while trying to secure acceptance can be seen in the record they compiled on four issues of central concern in the Reconstruction South.

The first of these was public education. In their Reconstruction constitutions, every state required that a tax-supported school system be set up for children of both races between the ages of five and twenty-one. This was a reform of great significance in a region where, with the possible exception of North Carolina, only a rudimentary system of public education had existed before the war and where only a fraction of the black school-age population—as little as 5 percent in Georgia—had been reached by the schools established by the missionary societies and the Freedmen's Bureau after Emancipation. The inauguration of these state systems was often delayed several years—even as late as 1872 in Georgia and 1873 in Alabama—because the legislatures had to work out the details of the school plan and then provide funding. Furthermore, schools had to be built and teachers trained and hired, the latter creating a special problem for black schools since the bureau teachers were now leaving and few whites wanted to take their place. Nevertheless, by the early 1870s, about half of the eligible children were enrolled in South Carolina and Mississippi and between 30 percent and 40 percent in Georgia and Alabama. By 1875, 2,500 schools were in operation in South Carolina, with about 130,000 students, while, in Mississippi, there were 4,650 schools and 168,000 children attending them, with blacks outnumbering whites in both states.

Impressive though these gains were, they could be construed rather differently. After all, these probably inflated figures indicated that most of the school-age children were still not enrolled, while those that did attend may not have been present with any regularity since attendance was not mandatory. Furthermore, the school year was limited to between four and six months, and the quality of instruction from frequently untrained and poorly educated teachers was questionable. Finally, the funds needed to start a statewide educational system were considerable, yet, not only was the amount appropriated barely adequate, it was rarely received. For example, about two-thirds of the Alabama appropriation never even reached the schools, while, in South Carolina, about a quarter of the designated amount was lost. Often, revenues earmarked for education were not collected adequately, as was the case with the poll tax in many states. Also legal fines designated for the schools were sometimes pocketed by the justices of the peace responsible for forwarding them to the treasury. But the greatest loss of revenue stemmed from the precipitous decline in land prices during the 1870s. This happened because the embryonic educational system was funded primarily from taxes on landed property.

Nevertheless, the foundations of southern public schooling were laid during Reconstruction. Although both races took advantage of the opportunities it offered, blacks in particular benefited from it considerably. By the end of the century, the black literacy rate had climbed to over 50 percent and a cadre of black teachers, ministers, and other professionals had emerged from the public schools as well as from the colleges, both public and private, that had been established during the postwar years.

Another major achievement of the period was the provision of civil rights protection and the outlawing of racial discrimination. In 1865 and 1866, southern legislatures had tried to create a separate legal category for the freedmen, akin to the status of the free Negro during slavery. But the federal occupation forces had rescinded these Black Codes. Congress had then enacted its Civil Rights Act of 1866, which required that states guarantee equal protection under the law. Once the Republicans gained control in the South, this federal initiative was followed up with antidiscrimination clauses in the new constitutions and with laws prescribing penalties for individuals who violated the civil rights of others. Of these enactments, the most rigorous was South Carolina's act of 1868, which imposed a fine of $1,000 or a year's imprisonment for owners of businesses who discriminated; it also required the accused to demonstrate his innocence rather than the victim to prove his guilt, a procedure that no other civil rights law has ever demanded.

Despite this legislation, discrimination continued to occur. It was virtually institutionalized in the schools since, with blacks concurring, the state laws had avoided the problematic issue of making integration mandatory. Only in Louisiana was mixing required. But the result there was that, in the back-country parishes, whites resisted the introduction of public schools altogether, leaving just some sections of New Orleans with a mixed system. A similar reaction occurred when the Republicans insisted that state universities admit students of both races. Whites simply refused for many years to apply, while, in Mississippi, for example, a separate college was created for blacks, called Alcorn University. In effect, public educational institutions were segregated as a matter of course.

In other areas of public life, however, black legislators demanded further action to prohibit discrimination. In particular, they focussed their attention on transportation where railroad, steamboat, and bus companies were instituting special compartments or carriages for black passengers. Fearing white outrage if differentiation on common carriers and in other public places were entirely eliminated, white Republicans, who themselves probably shared these misgivings about the desirability of racial mingling, either voted against proposed antidiscrimination measures or else yielded a weakened version which allowed for separate facilities provided they were not obviously inferior in quality. But blacks and more radical whites were tenacious, and they resisted the maneuvers and duplicity of the party leadership, which, in Mississippi in 1872, even went so far as to arrange that the draft of an extensive civil rights measure be conveniently lost. A year later, however, the opposition in Mississippi and in most other states was forced to capitulate, with the result that thoroughgoing legislation was enacted that prohibited discrimination in public places. This concession was yielded because black lawmakers and their constituents were demanding antidiscrimination laws as an earnest of the party's commitment and, by 1873, the Republicans had to acknowledge that, since they had failed in their quest for white support, they were now thoroughly dependent on blacks and had therefore to propitiate them.

In the area of race relations, the thrust of Reconstruction was quite clearly toward equal rights and nondiscrimination and away from the subordination of slavery. Not only were laws passed providing for equal treatment, but blacks also were employed in police forces and fire departments and they held public office, to some degree, at all levels of government. Nevertheless, patterns of racial separation persisted and the Republicans moved reluctantly to eliminate them. It was perhaps too much to expect that, only a few years after the ending of black slavery, a political party that was led by men like Governor James L. Alcorn of Mississippi, who at his inauguration held two separate public receptions, one for blacks and the other for whites, could act vigorously to erase racial distinctions and barriers.

Indeed, blacks themselves were often unwilling to force the issue. As already noted, they accepted segregation in the schools because insistence on mixing might have jeopardized the entire system. Equally, blacks frequently withdrew to form their own institutions and associations when confronted with attempts to discriminate against or subordinate them. The most important instance of this occurred in religion. Not only did blacks set up independent congregations under their own ministers and deacons, but they even formed separate conferences to organize black churches within a particular denomination, such as the Baptists or the Methodists. But the black church was not anomalous; it stood at the center of a network of black institutions of all kinds, ranging from self-help and benevolent associations to social and fraternal societies. Thus, the post-Emancipation years witnessed the emergence among blacks of a separate and independent community, particularly in the cities and towns where it was possible to build group strength as well as forge an ethnic and cultural identity.

Nevertheless, because discriminatory practices were so widespread, some historians have assumed that there was no significant improvement in southern race relations during Reconstruction. In his study of blacks in Reconstruction South Carolina, entitled *After Slavery* (1965), Joel Williamson even went so far as to conclude that "separation had crystallized into a comprehensive pattern which, in its essence, remained unaltered until the middle of the twentieth century." But this view is far too pessimistic. Admittedly, the gains that blacks made during the postwar years were, in some respects, disappointing, while white antipathy and discrimination underwent little, if any, change. All the same, civil rights laws were placed on the statute books of the southern states and hundreds of blacks held offices of public trust. Reconstruction may not have broken down racial barriers and ended discrimination, but it was certainly an era of improvement in southern race relations. As Howard Rabinowitz's *Race Relations in the Urban South, 1865–1890* (1979) demonstrated, it was an unquestionable advance over the total exclusion from white institutions that blacks had experienced during slavery. Equally, it was a far cry from what would transpire later, in the 1890s, when white hostility became unbridled and a system of legalized racial segregation was imposed that was to last for three-quarters of a century. Set in this context, race relations during Reconstruction were clearly improving and, even though blacks obtained only half a loaf, it was a gain that seemed, at the time, to be preferable to nothing. This more optimistic assessment also made it possible for blacks to anticipate that, after a while, once whites became used to blacks being free, their attitudes might change for the better. Despite its shortcomings, Reconstruction was therefore an era of hope and advancement in southern race relations.

Optimism was also the mood which permeated the Republican party as it embarked on its program of internal improvements, in particular the building of railroads. This was the third of the major issues tackled by the Republicans, and it was the one about which they were the most confident.

Throughout the region, a clamorous demand, amounting almost to a mania, had arisen after the war for the creation of a system of railroads as the key element in the revival of the southern economy. Railroads, it was thought, would not only produce prosperity, but they would also bring about economic development and usher in what was being referred to as the "New South." If the Republicans could meet this demand successfully, the party's prospects would be enormously enhanced, if not guaranteed. Every community that was invigorated by the arrival of the railroad would be indebted to the party, while the economic revival that the railroads were expected to generate would demonstrate the credibility and effectiveness of the Republican regimes, particularly among the financial interests of the South. As the Jackson, Mississippi, *Pilot* observed in 1871, legislation to promote railroads "will prove to the thinking people that the great Republican party is one of progress, of energy, of principles founded upon good, sound common sense." In addition, by giving priority to economic development and railroad building, the competing factions and constituencies within the party could be mollified because the policy would almost certainly benefit, not just one particular sector, but the population as a whole. Thus, state aid to railroads could not fail to benefit the region as well as the party, and so it was pursued with a vigor and an enthusiasm that was breathtaking.

Railroads were the centerpiece of Republican lawmaking from the moment the party gained power in 1868. For the next three or four years, countless bills to aid railroads were introduced and passed in the legislatures of the southern states. General railway laws were enacted, providing for specified amounts of aid upon completion of each mile of track. These were followed by separate bills committing state support to particular lines. Usually, the aid was in the form, not of an outright cash subsidy, but of an official endorsement of a company's bonds. With government backing, these bonds gained credibility and thus became more readily marketable. In exchange for this aid, the state was given a lien on the road, should the latter default on payments to its stockholders. While historians have always been aware of the Republicans' involvement in railroad construction, they have not recognized how deeply entangled the party was or how essential to its prospects was the success of this policy. In fact, it has been argued recently, by Mark Summers in his *Railroads, Reconstruction and the Gospel of Prosperity: Aid under the Radical Republicans, 1865–1877* (1984), that railroads were so important to the Republicans that they staked their party's future on them and, in the process, overcommitted themselves. But it was a risky venture because, when the railroads ran into difficulties—as they soon did—a series of disasters resulted which so totally embarrassed the party that it was overwhelmed and ultimately ruined.

So insistent and numerous were the railroads' demands for aid and so eager were the inexperienced Republicans to grant it that the enactment of railroad bills became almost an obsession. By 1870, this prompted Edwin Belcher, a black Republican legislator from Georgia, to suggest mockingly that the party had better make provision for the day that was imminent when there would be no land left in the state on which to build more railroads. To forestall this crisis, he introduced a resolution asking the "United States government for permission to construct railroads in Alaska, and that we be allowed to extend state aid to the same." Despite its sarcasm, Belcher's proposal nonetheless exposed the lack of restraint that characterized Republican railroad policy. Roads were promoted indiscriminately without overall planning and frequently without determining whether the company that was to receive aid was properly run and financially sound. Republican legislators were also careless about protecting their state's liability, since they often ignored laws that already existed for the regulation of government aid to internal improvements. This lack of precaution was then aggravated by the unanticipated reluctance on the part of both the federal government and private northern capital to promote southern railroads. As a result, the southern states were utterly helpless when, as soon happened, the region's railroads found themselves overextended and unable to pay their creditors.

The Republicans' forays into economic development and railroad finance were also thwarted by their political opponents. Interestingly, the Democrats were not unalterably opposed to railroads. Instead, their stance was one of ambivalence and deception. On the one hand, they wanted the economy to revive and be developed. In fact, they had passed railway laws themselves in 1865 and 1866 before the Republicans took over. On the other hand, they had no intention of allowing their despised rivals to succeed and thereby gain the acceptance they so desperately needed. To accommodate these contradictory aims, Democratic legislators stood aside while Republican majorities passed the railroad legislation, thereby managing to disassociate themselves from a policy they actually approved. Once the laws went into operation, however, the Democratic party as a whole was quick to attack shortcomings in their implementation. They charged the Republicans with extravagance for their excessively liberal extension of the public credit; with imprudence because of their failure to safeguard the interests of the state; with favoritism in their choice of which lines to subsidize; and with corruption for being so open to pecuniary influence from importunate company lobbyists. Besides denigrating the mechanics of the policy in this way, the Democrats also undermined the financing of it by besmirching the reputation of the Republican governments, thereby purposefully making it difficult for them to sell state bonds and obtain loans. Since the entire state aid policy was based on credit, this weakening of public confidence was devastating. The result was that, within a few years, when most of the roads found themselves unable to pay their way, the whole financial edifice collapsed. This disaster was further aggravated by the catastrophic failure in the North late in 1873 of the highly respected banking house of Jay Cooke which had, in parallel fashion, overextended itself in railroad investments, specifically the Northern Pacific.

The party's ignominy was compounded by the realization

that only 7,000 miles of track, 2,000 in Texas alone, had been constructed. Moreover, it had often been laid without coordination or any wider planning. Nevertheless, when added to the track that had already been built before the war, it could be argued that the initial foundations for a regional railroad network had been laid. But the price for this still debatable proposition was that the southern states had been saddled with millions of dollars of debt. The precise amount of it is difficult to ascertain since most of it was in the form of endorsements, categorized as "contingent debt." Republicans tried to claim that this kind of debt was not an actual and incurred liability. But that was simply rhetoric, since the states had liens on the property of the defaulting roads and neither the mortgage nor the assets could now find a buyer. At any rate, public funds would have to be used to pay off these liabilities, which increased the states' indebtedness and put further strain on their already inadequate revenues.

The Republicans' record on the issue of land and labor, the fourth and final area of party policy to be examined, was also disappointing. After the party took office, the possibility of making land available for the freedmen disappeared from public discussion. Apart from the creation of South Carolina's land commission in 1868, nothing was done. Even when state governments later seized land for nonpayment of taxes, the property was never used as a resource for setting blacks up as homesteaders. In fact, the land was not even readily available to whites. For instance, six million acres, or about 20 percent, of the land in Mississippi was forfeited by 1875, yet nearly all of it was returned to the original owners after payment of minimal penalties. This was the outcome because alternative purchasers could not be found who had the means to buy and because the state obviously ruled out the possibility of making it available to the landless, blacks in particular.

The result was that, during Reconstruction, virtually all the freedmen worked as laborers. Since the Freedmen's Bureau was being phased out in 1868 when the Republicans assumed power, the new governments proceeded to pass legislation that would both encourage these laborers to commit themselves to sign contracts with employers and protect them in case they were not paid. These measures took the form of laborer's lien laws intended to secure the laborer's interests through a lien against his employer on the crop that was about to be grown. But the laws were designed to fortify the precarious system of farming on credit that was emerging after the war. Their purpose was therefore not just to defend the laborer, who was after all only one of its component parts. Because of this, the employer's lien for supplies advanced on credit to the laborer was also secured. Since this lien was invariably superior to the laborer's, the employer was reimbursed first. He was also penalized less severely if he broke the contract because a defaulting employee forfeited, without any compensation, the entire crop he had planted. Lastly, since taking his employer to court necessitated hiring a lawyer and facing unsympathetic white judges and juries, blacks, who were the majority of the laborers, could rarely resort to this remedy.

The Republicans' lien legislation did little, therefore, to protect plantation laborers. Meanwhile, a system of labor emerged and became entrenched that was ultimately to prove quite damaging to the prospects of southern labor in the post-Emancipation era. Although it was not uniform in its terms and conditions, this labor system, known generally as sharecropping, provided for the hiring of the laborer under a year-long contract to work a designated plot of land on his employer's farm. The latter supplied tools, seed, and a cabin, and paid the cropper with a share, usually half, of the crop he produced. So satisfactory was this solution to the problems besetting southern agriculture in the wake of the war and Emancipation that it was widely adopted, not only in the plantation areas where slaves had earlier been the labor force, but in the upcountry as well.

In the beginning, the system grew out of the labor contract arrangement that the Freedmen's Bureau had settled on as an interim measure for getting the plantations back into operation without delay. The year-long contract enabled employers to secure a stable and sufficient supply of labor throughout the entire crop cycle, as they had done under slavery. When the stipulation was added that payment was to be in kind rather than in cash, which was virtually nonexistent in the postwar South, the foundations of sharecropping had been laid and the employers' two most essential needs had been met.

Initially, these provisions were not unacceptable to the laborer. They fell short naturally of the acquisition of land, but by 1867, certainly by 1868, that was clearly out of the question. Also out of reach for most freedmen was the chance to become a tenant and rent their own land and provide their own implements and supplies, because they just did not have the means to obtain these items for themselves. Although less desirable than either of these two possibilities, the alternative of being a cropper who was paid in shares and who was responsible for the operation and the product of his assigned land was nevertheless relatively attractive. It was certainly better than being a slave and was probably preferable to working as a rootless day laborer or as part of a closely supervised gang.

In time, however, the degree of independence that sharecropping offered began to evaporate. With no means available to them to purchase goods before the crop was harvested, croppers were forced to rely on a local merchant or their employer to advance them food, clothing, and other supplies. But the interest rates they charged were usurious—rarely less than 20 percent. Since the cropper's loan was unsecured, the rate was bound to be high in a region where the lack of currency and capital made credit scarce and therefore expensive anyway. The cropper's indebtedness became even more acute when, in the 1870s, the price for his crop, which was invariably cotton, plummeted. This decline was caused mainly by overproduction of the nonperishable yet readily available commodity once it had become, in essence, the medium of exchange in the credit-starved South. Cotton was grown as collateral and as payment for loans, but its loss of value made those debts even more expensive and onerous. Thus, in a financial chain that was based on the bartering of supplies in exchange for cotton, the weakest link was the cropper. He had nothing to bargain with but his labor and the crop he had not yet harvested.

While this repressive labor system was developing, changes were also occurring in the region's pattern of land tenure. At one time, historians thought that the plantations of the South were broken up after the war. This verdict was based on wishful thinking as well as on a simple error in interpreting the postwar censuses. Admittedly, the size of southern farms had changed dramatically. Most cultivated land was now being operated as family farms, while only a small fraction of units, about 5.3 percent, planted more than 100 acres in crops. The infrequency of the large-scale plantation did not, however, mean that land-ownership had been dispersed. Instead, what had happened was that the owners of these large units had retained possession but had simply rented them out to a number of tenants whom the census takers had incorrectly designated as owners.

In recent years, historians have confirmed this assessment through local studies of, for example, Alabama's western black belt and the counties of the Natchez district on the Mississippi River. They have concluded not only that a small percentage of owners held on to most of the land but that, to a great extent, the families which had possessed large holdings of 1,000 acres or more before the war persisted as members of this elite into the 1870s. They were able to do this mainly because the economic stringency of the times made it extremely difficult for others to buy their land. But they had also to resort to imaginative financial maneuvering, for instance, arranging the purchase or transfer of property among friends and relations in order to avoid losing it through enforced sale or by default for nonpayment of taxes. In the cotton-growing areas, there was therefore little change in the pattern of landholding, certainly among the elite. On the other hand, the way that cotton was grown altered dramatically as the large unitary plantation became decentralized into small plots run by tenants and croppers.

In the upcountry, unlike the black belt, plantations had never predominated. Also land use had been more varied;

growers of cotton for sale had coexisted with farmers subsisting on their own food crops and with herdsmen grazing their own livestock, mainly hogs, on the common lands. Despite these differences, a similar pattern was developing in the postwar years, according to Steven Hahn's study of the Georgia piedmont, *The Roots of Populism* (1983). Small tenant-farms began to proliferate, landlessness grew, and agricultural wealth continued to be concentrated, possibly even increasing. This occurred primarily because the yeoman farmers who had earlier predominated in these regions proved unable to recover from the short food crops and declining cotton prices after the war, with the result that most of them had to sell their land. In the following decade, a parallel loss befell the herdsmen. They were driven off their pastures because of the fence laws that ended the open range by requiring that graziers enclose their livestock. The instigators of the fence laws and the chief beneficiaries of the yeomen's loss of land were the more successful cotton growers. Because of these developments, they not only acquired more acres but gained access to an increasing supply of landless laborers as well. Also benefiting from the small farmers' difficulties were the merchants who advanced them their supplies and controlled their credit. Whenever farmers could not repay their debts—as often happened because of the overproduction of cotton and its resultant drop in price—the merchants found themselves in the position of being able to seize their land. Thus, changes were occurring, but they led away from a diversified subsistence economy toward a system of commercial agriculture, with cotton the exclusive crop and landless tenants and sharecroppers the primary work force. Indeed, this was the trend throughout the region during Reconstruction. A series of new practices and structures were emerging in response to postwar economic and social pressures, and there was little the Republicans could have done to alter the outcome.

Nevertheless, while it had been in power during Reconstruction, the party had embarked on a number of policies intended to change southern priorities. It had managed, with some degree of success, to create a system of mass public education. It had taken action to alter prevailing patterns of racial discrimination. It had promoted economic development, in particular the building of railroads. And, finally, the party had assisted in the emergence of a new system of free labor. Moreover, these were not minor matters; they challenged the region's past practices and assumptions frontally. That meant, however, that success was not very likely. If two conditions had been present at the time, the Republicans might have made more headway. First, the region had to have the capital and currency at hand that was needed to underwrite these innovations. And, second, the Republicans themselves had to have solid political strength and a progressive cast of mind if they were to be able to implement them. Since neither was in fact available, the outcome was predictable. In effect, the task was simply beyond the resources and capacity of the party, and even of the region as a whole.

CHAPTER THREE

Declining Influence: Redemption, 1874–1879

Collapse in the South

In the reconstructed South, there were two political parties but no two-party system. This was because one of the existing parties refused to accord legitimacy to the other. The opponents of Reconstruction, that is, the Democrats, would not acknowledge that the Republican party had a right to participate in southern political life. First of all, it was the partisan instrument of a Reconstruction policy that had been framed and imposed by a northern Congress and, second, its support was based essentially on the votes of the former slaves.

This denial of legitimacy was even more serious because it extended beyond the political party to encompass state government as well, since the Republicans controlled and ran it. This amounted to a renunciation of the authority of the state. In effect, the Republicans were viewed as an occupying force whose authority was rejected. Nevertheless, because they were a political party, not an army, they had to govern by consent. Thus, they had to obtain legitimacy, and this would only be

done by breaking down disrespect and converting it into political support at election time. As evidence that legitimacy
was indeed the issue at stake, historians have customarily categorized these Republican administrations as "regimes" and
their defeat as their "overthrow," descriptive terms not applicable under normal circumstances.

From the outset, the Republicans worked energetically to
acquire legitimacy. They lavished attention and patronage on
politically prominent white Southerners who, despite the risk
of shame or censure, chose to affiliate with the suspect new
party. Indeed, so eager was the party to please them as well
as advertise their defection that many were given the most
prestigious positions it could bestow. Some were even appointed chief justice of the state supreme court, like Joseph E.
Brown in Georgia, Richmond Pearson in North Carolina, and
Samuel Rice in Alabama, while others such as Mississippi's
James L. Alcorn, Alabama's William H. Smith, and Georgia's
Rufus Bullock became governor. Also, the Republicans' policy
of railroad building was pursued with an almost obsessive
determination and generosity because it was thought to be the
"open sesame" to success and respectability. By contrast, the
party leadership quickly relented on policies that would have
been punitive to well-to-do whites, like land redistribution and
political proscription. And, finally, the party tried to disarm
white opposition with reassurances about the limited role and
influence of blacks within its ranks.

The Republicans did not abandon their search for respectability, even after their railroad policy collapsed in the
mid-1870s and immersed the party in debt and disgrace. The
Democrats' assault on Republican extravagance and fiscal ir-
responsibility was immediately met with regrets and with
promises of reform. The party offered to consolidate and scale
down the state debt, cut government expenses, and reduce
taxation. Thus, retrenchment and reform became the watch-
word by 1874, as Governors Elisha Baxter in Arkansas, Daniel
Chamberlain in South Carolina, David Lewis in Alabama,
Adelbert Ames in Mississippi, and William P. Kellogg in Lou-

isiana, all admitted past error and tried to refute Democratic claims that they were incompetent and fiscally irresponsible.

This concern about their capacity to govern had also been at issue in 1870–71 when the Ku Klux Klan was in operation, intimidating Republican voters and sometimes assassinating party leaders. This, of course, was not the first appearance of the Klan. It had already revealed its effectiveness as a local terrorist organization in the elections of 1868. But, after a period of quiescence in the wake of its failure to defeat Reconstruction and deny Grant the presidency, it emerged again. At first, Republican governors tried to ignore the problem for fear that drawing attention to it would simply prove that their party's authority was contested. Then, after that approach proved ineffective, they would put the burden of taking care of lawlessness on the shoulders of the officials in the county where the disturbances were taking place. Finally, if that did not work, they often obtained policing authority from the legislature and took judicial and coercive action themselves.

The problem with taking vigorous measures against the Klan and other outbreaks of violence was that the consequences were almost certain to be damaging. Even if successful, the police action was likely to be seen as evidence of an inability to govern without force. Typical of this was what happened in North Carolina in 1870 after Governor William Holden had virtually waged war on the Klan in the piedmont counties of Caswell and Alamance. The Democrats immediately accused him of introducing military rule and destroying civil liberties, a charge sufficiently persuasive to defeat Holden's party in the legislative elections that summer. There was, however, one exception. In the winter of 1868–69, a military countermove by Governor Powell Clayton in Arkansas was carried out successfully and without serious political repercussions. This action was probably effective, not only because Clayton took steps quickly and without fear of the Democrats' reaction, but because his militia was largely composed of whites.

Elsewhere, a loyal Republican militia would be overwhelmingly black, with the result that governors became paralyzed by fear that military action would degenerate into racial warfare, an outcome more dreaded than the disorder already occurring. Yet, of course, the victims of the violence and intimidation were Republican supporters, mainly blacks, and the aim behind it all was to undermine the Republican party. That this was the intent is extremely likely because, as Allen Trelease's detailed investigation of the Klan, called *White Terror* (1971), concluded, the Klan's operations were most vigorous in those counties, mainly the piedmont, where Republican control was vulnerable owing to the closeness of the racial balance in the population. Although attempts by local whites to control blacks socially and economically may also have been involved, the Klan's overall aim was almost certainly political. And political violence presented the Republicans with a terrible dilemma, as those who fomented it were well aware.

Indeed, the Republicans' entire political situation was an agonizing dilemma. They sought legitimacy and white acceptance, yet every step they took to protect their organization and their predominantly black supporters served only to confirm their ineligibility. Measures to put down disorder and mobilize the militia were denounced as arbitrary. Laws to protect voters from intimidation were criticized as partisan. And attempts to reward blacks with offices or enact antidiscrimination laws were interpreted as evidence that the party was beholden to its black followers. No Republican was more forceful in attempting to protect his party than Henry C. Warmoth, a Union soldier from Illinois who stayed in the South after the war and who, in 1868, at the age of twenty-six, was elected governor of Louisiana. In the legislative session of 1869–70, the New Orleans Metropolitan Police was made into a large and up-to-date force with a jurisdiction extending well beyond the city. In addition, a sizable state militia, commanded by the celebrated Confederate general, James Longstreet, was formed, consisting of 5,000 men who were then divided into black and white units. Finally, an election returning board was created which was manned by the three top-ranking executive officers of the state and empowered to reject ballots from districts where intimidation had occurred. Yet this assertion of power, rather than quelling opposition, simply provoked it on a massive scale. At the same time, it demonstrated that the party had to rely for its survival on extraordinary and questionable measures. Accordingly, Louisiana became an armed camp during Reconstruction, and the Republicans, barely able to govern, failed more completely than in any other state to secure recognition and acceptance.

The unresolved dilemma of whether the party was better served by conciliation than by coercion also shaped the factional divisions which arose within it. These factions were pervasive and virulent and they contributed significantly to the party's weakness. Historians no longer attribute Republican factionalism to a quarrelsomeness or lust for power peculiar to the party's southern branch, but they do wonder whether there might have been features in its basic structure and composition that produced them. As a new and hastily formed party, perhaps it lacked the organizational discipline and hierarchy capable of curbing internal rivalries. Or possibly it was the existence of three quite distinct groups in the party that were already divided by racial and regional identities that accounted for the divisions. Whatever the cause, these factions split the Republicans apart. Invariably, there were two groups and they aligned according to party strategy, one urging conciliation and legitimacy, the other organizational consolidation and military protection. This was the case, for instance, in the rivalry between the factions headed by James Alcorn and Adelbert Ames in Mississippi, between the followers of Willard Warner and George Spencer in Alabama, and between those loyal to Joseph Brooks and Powell Clayton in Arkansas. Usually, the natives were influential in the conciliationist group, while Northerners and blacks sided with its rival whose priority was to protect the party's base. Thus, the Republicans' strategic quandary became even more problematic as it took on an organizational form in the factional divisions that were plaguing the party.

The factional struggle was frequently so intense that it

produced an open split in the party's ranks, resulting in one group bolting and running independently. Since the party's hold on power was so precarious anyway, it is puzzling that its members could act so destructively. That they were able to do so was evidently because the Republican organization was unable to exert effective control. Like its hold on power, its influence over its supporters was weak. Also Republicans may have been prepared to take such drastic action because they shared the Democrats' view that their own party lacked legitimacy and authority and so could be defied readily and with impunity. Perhaps they also calculated that the party's life-span was likely to be brief and, if so, they did not want to be tied too closely to it. At any rate, bolts occurred frequently and resulted in temporary electoral alliances with the party's opponents, the Democrats. Invariably, since they were already more active in appealing to non-Republicans, it was the conciliationist faction that bolted and engaged in fusion with the Democrats.

These fusion arrangements took place mainly at the local level, though on occasion in statewide campaigns. In 1872 bolting Republicans fused with Democrats throughout the South. This coincided with the split at the national level when the Liberal Republicans broke away from the regular party organization and ran a separate ticket. With Horace Greeley, the editor of the *New York Tribune*, as their presidential candidate, the Liberals disassociated themselves from the Grant administration, because of its corruption and its failure to bring about sectional peace and reconciliation. Their demand for governmental reform and a more lenient approach to white Southerners also proved attractive to scalawags who were dissatisfied with the party in the South. Simultaneously, the prospect of a serious split among their Republican opponents was welcomed by the Democrats in both sections. The upshot was that the Democrats endorsed Greeley as their own presidential candidate, even though he was well-known as a life-long hater of their party. Meanwhile, throughout the South, Democrats fused with bolting Republicans to form bipartisan coalitions campaigning at the state level for reform and retrenchment.

The result of the national election was a resounding triumph for the Republicans over this anomalous marriage of convenience. In the South, too, the Republicans won, but their victory was bittersweet. They held on to power but, in the process, lost forever most of their native white support, which had seen the Democrats' endorsement of the bolting Republicans as the opportunity to disengage and rejoin the critics of Reconstruction. As a result, the Republican party was thrown back onto its black constituency, a reliance that was becoming increasingly evident since many Northerners were, by this time, also giving up on the party and even leaving the South. Therefore, after 1872, the Republicans had to acknowledge that they had failed both to harmonize the party's discordant elements and to build a base among the white population. The moment of truth had arrived; southern Republicanism was, as its opponents had always charged, essentially a black man's party.

Besides its own internal difficulties and shortcomings, the Republican party was beset by a relentless foe. After the war, the former Confederates had fought for over two years to reject, or at least evade, the terms proposed by the victorious North. They had tried to maneuver around Johnson's policy in 1865; they had flatly rejected Congress' Fourteenth Amendment a year later; and they had attempted to undermine the requirements of the Reconstruction Act from 1867 to 1868. Although failing to avert Reconstruction, their resistance did, nevertheless, make Congress' task extremely difficult. Paradoxically, however, their refusal to accept these proposals forced Congress to introduce terms that were increasingly severe. Finally, in 1868, a last desperate attempt to forestall Reconstruction was made when, with the Klan operating unofficially and independently as a weapon of last resort, they mobilized all their political resources to prevent the election of Ulysses Grant.

In Georgia and Louisiana, they were successful, although at a cost of about 1,000 lives in the Louisiana election alone, according to the report of the Ku Klux Klan Investigating

Committee of 1871. This questionable feat was not enough, however, since Grant was elected president and every southern state was reconstructed and came under Republican control. Accordingly, the Democrats—as the anti-Reconstructionists had begun to identify themselves—had to reassess their strategy. In a dramatic about-face after 1868, they decided to eschew confrontation and try instead to defeat the Republicans in the normal competition of party politics—that is, by winning electoral majorities peacefully. Behind this judgment was the conviction that continued resistance could only keep the region in a state of political turmoil detrimental to its social stability and economic recovery. Persistent confrontation would also force the federal government to intervene constantly in southern affairs, while simultaneously scaring off much-needed northern capital. This change of course, which paralleled a similar shift by the national Democrats in 1871, was called the New Departure. Under it, the party accepted the finality of Reconstruction and acknowledged the actuality of black suffrage.

Their accommodation to the new political order in the South enabled the Democrats to become involved in the emerging political and economic developments of the region. Since they could no longer be dismissed as out-of-touch obstructionists, the Democrats hoped to attract support from economic and financial interests that might otherwise have been won over by the Republicans because of their promotion of internal improvements as well as their ties to the federal authorities and to northern capital. Also, former Whigs who might have resisted affiliation with their prewar political enemies, particularly if the Democrats were disruptive and resistant to change, would reconsider. Besides helping to retain white support, the New Departure provided a means of making inroads into the Republicans' black constituency. This may appear a rather unlikely proposition, but the Democrats had great hopes for it. By their acceptance of the right of blacks to vote, the party might no longer be seen as unalterably opposed to the political gains made by the freedmen. Moreover, as their employers, Democrats could bring pressure on the ex-slaves to realize that, politically, their best interests lay in appeasing their bosses rather than antagonizing them by voting Republican. So Zebulon B. Vance, the war-time governor of North Carolina, urged party members to "act so as to make them sick of the yankees, and show them that their old masters and themselves are natural allies." Meanwhile, the leading Democratic paper in the state, the Raleigh *Sentinel*, recommended that "Those who work daily with the negro can exercise great influence over him." If this maneuver were successful, two worrisome developments would be forestalled. Political parties would not be racially exclusive and the relations between white capital and black labor would not be aggravated by political polarization. To the Democrats, therefore, biracial parties could defuse the threat of racial friction posed by the introduction of the Republican party into the South.

The New Departure enabled the Democrats to stem the defection of whites, but it enticed only a smattering of blacks away from the Republicans. More effective at breaking down black support was the tactic of encouraging Republican dissension and then forming electoral alliances with factions of the party that bolted. Some black votes came with the bolters, but the main advantage of these fusion arrangements was that the Republicans were weakened by the split. In addition, the Democrats were benefited because they could disguise their identity in strong Republican districts through endorsement of and voting for bolting opposition candidates. Fusion and the New Departure had their greatest opportunity in 1872 with the Liberal Republican defection. But its disastrous outcome encouraged critics of the strategy within the party to demand yet another reconsideration of its priorities.

Thus commenced the third phase in the postwar struggle on the part of the region's traditional leaders to regain political control. The critics of the New Departure were described by contemporaries as Bourbons, not a reference to whiskey but to the French royal family that returned to the throne after Napoleon, having learned nothing and forgotten nothing. They insisted that the Democrats repudiate their recently adopted strategy of playing down the differences between the parties and accentuate instead their own party's distinctive identity, interests, and constituency. The New Departure, the Bourbons claimed, had tried to falsify the dichotomies in southern politics. In so doing, it had failed, not only to win over Republicans but, more seriously, to arouse the Democratic party's own supporters. The remedy was to shun fusion and to campaign instead as straight-out, unabashed Democrats. Simultaneously, the racial differences between the two parties were to be emphasized. With whites leaving the Republicans rapidly after 1872 and with blacks refusing to be lured by the Democrats, the reality of the racial polarization of southern politics seemed increasingly difficult to refute. So, after four years of obfuscation and evasion, race became politicized in 1873–74.

As campaign issues, race and white supremacy were extremely problematic for the Democrats, however. In states like Texas and Arkansas that had heavy white majorities, an appeal to race was not necessary because a well-organized straight-out campaign might win anyway. In fact, with the collapse of the Republicans' railroad schemes and the accompanying indebtedness, a focus on fiscal questions was as likely to succeed as race. Not only was it less disruptive but it was an issue with broad appeal that might encourage many Republicans to switch their vote because of dissatisfaction with their own party's economic record. Indeed, there is strong evidence that lower expenditures and therefore reduced taxes appealed to taxpayers regardless of party, since they were becoming very aware and angry that taxes had risen steeply under the Republicans. Particularly aggrieved were small landowners who paid significantly more now that the levy on slaves was abolished because the tax had been transferred to land. Since they were operating on a close margin anyway, the increased taxation pushed them to the brink. Therefore, it was quite probable that fiscal issues were more effective vote getters than race. Indeed, the Democrats captured Texas in 1873 and Arkansas in 1874 without basing their campaigns exclusively on white supremacy.

In those states where, by contrast, blacks were in a majority, a racial canvass seemed to guarantee defeat for the party of white supremacy. Indeed, that was the major reason why the Democrats had previously shied away from it. But the Bourbons conceived of race as an appeal so electrifying that it would rally whites who had previously been apathetic and confused when faced with the perplexing fusion politics of the New Departure. With their natural constituency stimulated and polling a full vote, they argued that the Democrats' chances would be considerably enhanced. The case for a race-based campaign was presented most graphically by Nathaniel B. Meade, a leader in James L. Kemper's successful straight-out canvass for governor of Virginia in 1873. "To save the state," he suggested, "we must make the issue *White and Black* race against race and the canvass red hot—the position must be made so odious that no decent white man can support the radical ticket and look a gentleman in the face." If, in addition, black Republicans could be intimidated into not voting, then victory was quite conceivable. Indeed, organized terror and intimidation was to be the military complement to the Bourbons' political strategy. Accordingly, the White League in Louisiana in 1874, the Rifle Clubs in Mississippi in 1875, and the Red Shirts in Wade Hampton's gubernatorial campaign of 1876 in South Carolina were mobilized to spread such fear among black Republicans that the party became demoralized.

In Louisiana, the White League attacked government buildings and assaulted officials in outlying Republican-held districts in order to shatter the party's local control. Two violent clashes revealed the bloody lengths to which organized terror would resort. One was at Colfax in Grant parish in 1873 when about one hundred blacks were murdered, most in cold blood, after their attempt to hold on to the besieged courthouse had failed. The other occurred at Coushatta in Red River parish, near Shreveport, a year later when six white Republican officials and two of their black associates were seized by a mob of a thousand whites from Coushatta and its vicinity. Despite promises to leave the town, they were all murdered by their captors, thereby eliminating the men who had run the parish under the leadership of a courageous Northerner, Marshall Twitchell, who, by chance, was not in town on the day of the massacre. Meanwhile, in New Orleans, the League fought a pitched battle with the Metropolitan Police and black militia at Liberty Place in September 1874. The Mississippi, Alabama, and South Carolina campaigns developed a common pattern of intimidation and violence. During the summer before the election, a racial affray was provoked in which blacks were attacked and hunted down as occurred at Clinton, Mississippi, in 1875 and at Hamburg, South Carolina, a year later. These incidents were followed by military drilling and nighttime terror in selected black counties. Meanwhile, Democratic politicians warned whites of their responsibility to their race for driving out the black man's party. So effective was this grim tactic in Alabama in 1874 that Walter Bragg, the Democratic state chairman, observed gloatingly: "The spirit of our people is roused to the highest pitch that will admit of control—the negroes sink down before it as if stricken with awe." With the Republicans staggering under these violent assaults and with whites responding eagerly to the Democrats' call for white supremacy, the outcome was the final defeat of Reconstruction in the Deep South states after 1874.

Drawing the color line between the two parties was the weapon that finally toppled the Republicans, as Michael Perman has shown in *The Road to Redemption: Southern Politics, 1869–1879* (1984). Since racial subordination was at the core of southern society and culture, race was obviously an ever-present element during Reconstruction, especially because the Republican party with its black constituency threatened to disturb the existing racial order. But, until the mid-1870s, the Democrats had deliberately chosen not to make race the issue dividing the two parties. Instead, they had relied on a strategy aimed at denying the Republican party credibility and legitimacy. With its northern origins and extensive black support in the South and with its far-from-perfect performance in office, there was plenty of ammunition available to keep the party off-balance and weaken it electorally. Besides, racial polarization was sure to provoke federal displeasure and intervention and also, quite probably, disrupt labor relations and frustrate economic revival. Thus, while it was understood that the parties were racial in essence, the Democrats were not willing to act upon this awareness politically. In actual fact, neither could the Republicans, because they were desperately eager to secure the votes and recognition of whites. Once it was clear that the Republicans could not attract a significant amount of white support, while, at the same time, it was apparent that the Democrats themselves could not win the Deep South without polling a greater white vote than they had previously been able to obtain, then it was both safe and necessary to play the race card.

As soon as the genie was out of the bottle, race became the issue defining the two parties, not only in those states where it had been employed as a last resort to redeem them from Republican rule, but throughout the entire region. Because theirs was the party that had uprooted Reconstruction and restored white supremacy, the Democrats now claimed what was tantamount to an unquestioned right to rule. But appearances were deceptive. After its return to power, the white man's party seemed to hesitate and belie its new, exultant identity. For it did not proceed right away to repeal the Republicans' civil rights legislation or to remove all black officials from power. The reason for the Democrats' reluctance was that a frontal assault was unnecessary. The Democrats had regained political dominance anyway and they did not need to vindicate their racial credentials by eradicating every gain that blacks had made under Reconstruction. Indeed, such action was almost certainly counterproductive, since it would provoke the federal authorities and also thwart the serious and effective overtures that, in a move reminiscent of the New Departure, the Democrats began making to reassure blacks and win over their votes. In effect, the Democratic leadership was concerned to quiet down the racial friction that had been generated during the "white supremacy" campaigns. Therefore, there was to be no further overt hostility toward blacks. Rather, they were to be reassured that the rule of white men "to the manor born" would be benevolent. As Governor Wade Hampton explained patronizingly to black South Carolinians in 1878, they had no reason to fear the return of the Democrats because "We propose to protect you and give you all your rights."

So there was no intention of removing blacks' legal rights, and they were accordingly left alone. Instead, other kinds of problems concerned the Democrats more. The first was the consolidation of the party's political control. This was achieved by the removal of the most important Republicans who still held office in the executive and judicial branches and by the reapportionment of the legislature so as to reduce Republican representation significantly. Then, in most states between 1874 and 1879, the Democrats called conventions to rewrite the Reconstruction constitutions of 1868. In these conventions, which they dominated, the Democrats prohibited the use of state aid for internal improvements and repudiated most of the debts incurred by the Republicans. In addition, the responsibilities and the cost of government were drastically reduced, as was the rate of taxation. Besides being a reaction against the presumed extravagance of Reconstruction, this initiative also represented a reassertion of the traditional laissez-faire, minimal government doctrines of the Democracy that were being urged on the party by its Bourbon purists. As it returned to power, the Democratic party was therefore also returning to its original identity and principles.

The third of the initiatives taken by the resurgent Democrats was their passage of laws aimed at tightening the existing controls over the plantation labor force. The target of this legislative activity was the modicum of autonomy that laborers, particularly black sharecroppers, still possessed under the newly emergent, but legally imprecise, labor system. A series of repressive ordinances gave landlords virtually uncontested control over their laborers. The first of these were laws prohibiting tenants and croppers from selling, without their employer's permission, the cotton they were growing on his land. The impact of these measures, called "sunset to sunrise" bills because they were intended to outlaw nighttime trading with local stores, was to prevent croppers from disposing of their share of the crop in whatever way and whenever they wished. Another step the state legislatures took drastically increased the severity of existing legal sanctions against theft and trespass. A third type of measure imposed restrictions on the laborer's ability to move around and bargain for better terms through what were called anti-enticement laws forbidding employers from competing for each other's workers. Frequently, states also levied taxes on labor agents in an attempt to curb their activity among the farm labor force. The ultimate device for ensuring the landlord's control over his laborers was the redrafting of the existing crop lien laws so as to give the landlord's lien for rent and supplies indisputable primacy over those of the laborer and, most important, of the merchant with whom the cropper may have been dealing for supplies and the sale of his cotton. By these measures, the landowners secured dominance over the post-Emancipation agricultural system and over the increasingly dependent labor force. Gone was the plantation worked by gangs of slaves. In its place, there had arisen a system that was repressive and labor-intensive and that, furthermore, possessed few of the features thought to be characteristic of free labor.

With the return of the Democrats to power in the late 1870s, the priorities of Reconstruction itself, not just the Republican party, had been substantially overthrown. As is invariably the case, however, the break with the recent past was not a clean one. Some of the features and priorities of Reconstruction persisted. The civil and political rights that blacks had won were retained on the statute books and would remain there until segregation and disfranchisement were made law at the turn of the century. Also a powerful segment of the Democratic party still pursued railroad building and pressed for the development of manufacturing, though neither could now expect public subsidization. But the discontinuities were far more noticeable, as the triumphant Democrats reduced governmental activism to a minimum, consolidated the region's repressive system of land and labor, and vindicated their claim to be the restorers of white supremacy. Reconstruction had pointed the way to a New South: its overthrow ensured that whatever was new about the South in the last quarter of the nineteenth century would be severely circumscribed by old practices and priorities.

Neglect in the North

While the edifice of Reconstruction was being dismantled by the southern Democrats, the federal government just watched from the sidelines. Its military presence was finally ended in 1877 after Rutherford B. Hayes had agreed to let the Democrats have control of the contested states of South Carolina, Louisiana, and Florida in exchange for those states' presidential vote. At the same time, there also seemed to be no compelling grounds for Washington's reinvolvement in southern affairs, since the new constitutions and labor laws did not infringe any federal statutes. All the same, this was a most puzzling development. How could northern Republicans allow these Reconstruction governments to collapse when they had labored with such zeal and at such risk to create them in the first place?

The federal government's inactivity was actually part of a process that had been set in motion several years earlier when the Grant administration had in effect decided to let the Reconstruction governments fend for themselves. In 1875 when Governor Ames of Mississippi had feared calling out the black militia and instead had sought military help from Washington, Attorney General Edwards Pierrepoint had responded icily that "the whole public are tired out with these annual, autumnal outbreaks in the South." Almost two years before this, Grant himself had expressed his contempt for the southern Republicans when he announced that "it is time for the republican party to unload. . . . I am done with them, and they will have to take care of themselves." He had then proceeded to cultivate dissident Republicans as well as to mollify dissatisfied Democrats so as to create a personal, nonpartisan following in anticipation of a third run for the presidency in 1876. This disassociation from the regular Republicans, coupled with his eagerness to please southern Democrats, caused him to take no action to save the failing Reconstruction governments in Texas in 1873 and Arkansas in 1874.

Although Grant became increasingly reluctant to intervene in the South after 1873 when he judged the Republican regimes neither capable nor worthy of being sustained, he had been quite involved from 1869 to 1872. This involvement had, however, lacked consistency and vigor, since, as William Gillette has argued in his *Retreat from Reconstruction, 1869–1879* (1979), the president had no clearly defined objective in his dealings with the South. Instead, his actions were usually determined by specific circumstances or by his own political needs and those of the national party. Furthermore, whenever he did act, he began with relative firmness but soon backed off, leaving his southern allies sometimes more vulnerable than before he had intervened.

Presidential action took several forms. The first was political. Grant intervened in Virginia and Mississippi in 1869 to have Confederate disfranchisement removed from the new constitutions. That same year, he helped rescue the Republican government in Georgia by commencing Reconstruction anew, only to withdraw when Governor Bullock wanted to prolong the state's reliance on Washington. Then, in the 1872 elections, he sided unequivocally with the regular party in the South in its campaign against the dissident Liberal Republicans, a stance which of course aided his own reelection prospects. Another kind of involvement was military. Sometimes he sent troops to put down disorder, as in North Carolina's armed struggle with the Klan in 1870. At other times, federal forces were dispatched to restore calm when violence threatened to erupt over a contest for control of a legislative body, such as occurred in Alabama after its disputed election of 1872. A third type of intervention was undertaken to supervise federal elections and thereby enforce the Fifteenth Amendment, which provided for universal suffrage. This happened on a number of occasions during Reconstruction, though it did not necessarily require that troops be dispatched.

Of all these various actions, the most successful was the military and judicial campaign to round up and try members of the Klan in the South Carolina piedmont region in 1870–71. Less effective, though certainly Grant's most persistent intervention, was his involvement in Louisiana. Time and again, he sent troops in to quell antigovernment violence as well as to maintain the Republican party in power. He even became embroiled in the factional dispute that pitted Governor Warmoth's wing of the party against the Custom House group, headed by James Casey, Grant's brother-in-law. The president's continual intrusion into Louisiana politics enabled the Republican administration under Governor William P. Kellogg to hold on to power from 1872 to 1876, but, at the same time, the party's reliance on periodic federal support in an emergency discouraged it from settling its own internal problems and coming to terms with its political opponents. Meanwhile, the spectacle of the federal government's unseemly involvement in factional squabbles among the Republicans themselves served only to diminish its authority, as did its continual entanglement in Louisiana's serpentine politics.

The deficiencies in the president's southern policy cannot, however, be explained solely by Grant's own shortcomings. They reflected instead the ambivalence, and even reluctance, that Northerners in general felt about involvement in southern Reconstruction. At first glance, it might seem that a problem of such magnitude that had provoked a governmental crisis from 1865 to 1868 would have made the American people absolutely determined that what had been done in the South had to succeed. That was not, however, the case. There were concerns, attitudes, and interests in the North that, from the outset, militated against a wholehearted engagement in Reconstruction. Thus, the collapse of Reconstruction was not attributable simply to the gradual waning of an earlier commitment, as many Revisionist historians concluded a century later. Rather, there were serious reservations, and even opposition, from the very beginning.

These obstacles were numerous, but four in particular will suffice to point out the cross-pressures operating on northern policymakers. The first of them was the North's racism. Just as the war had not been waged to free blacks from slavery, Reconstruction was not intended to make blacks equal. Whatever equality they did obtain during Reconstruction was, like Emancipation, a by-product, not an objective. The federal officials responsible for southern policy came from a society where racial prejudice was an accepted norm and where racial discrimination in all areas of life was legally sanctioned and universally practiced. Leon Litwack's definitive study of blacks in the North in the first half of the nineteenth century, entitled *North of Slavery* (1961), concluded with the observation that "In virtually every phase of existence, Negroes found themselves systematically separated from whites." Even more forthright was the view of a contemporary, the radical Republican congressman from Indiana, George W. Julian. In a public speech in 1865, he declared: "the trouble is that *we hate the negro.*"

Emancipation, therefore, presented to white Northerners as well as Southerners the fearsome specter of the unleashing of four million blacks. This was not only a far greater number than the 250,000 already living in the North, but these blacks, unlike their northern counterparts, were illiterate and had never experienced freedom and autonomy. Northern white fear of the consequences of abolition had in fact surfaced before the war when it had been perhaps the greatest stumbling block the abolitionists had had to face. Lincoln too had agonized over this same problem and, in his annual message of December 1864, had proposed a solution in the form of a detailed plan for the overseas colonization of the slaves after they had been liberated. But, because of its enormous cost and because ex-

slaves were the only available source of labor for the plantations, black removal was considered impractical. The need for
the freedmen as laborers resulted in the rejection of another
possibility that was broached at the time. This was the idea
embodied in Sherman's Field Order No. 15 for blacks to be
restricted to specified enclaves, there to live and develop separately.

If blacks could not be isolated from whites either by colonization or by separate development, then there was nothing
to stop them from migrating to the North. Of course, laws
could be passed prohibiting them from entering northern states,
but a far better disincentive was to make it more attractive
for the freedmen to stay in the South. As Senator Roscoe Conkling of New York told the Joint Committee on Reconstruction in 1866, the most effective way to prevent blacks from
"bursting in hordes upon the North" was to "give them liberty
and rights in the South, and they will stay there and never
come into a cold climate to die." Although Conkling's state-
ment ran counter to the irrefutable evidence that blacks had
no difficulty surviving in the inclement North, it revealed
nevertheless that the need to keep blacks in the South was
evidently a stimulus toward formulating a Reconstruction policy that would give them justice and protection where they
were already. Such a policy would also meet another need
perceived by the North, which was to ensure that enough labor
was at hand to revive southern agriculture. Thus, justice and
northern self-interest could both be satisfied.

When the specifics of northern policies toward the freedmen were discussed, talk always focussed on what their "position" in southern society should be. In itself, this inquiry
about their proper place was evidence of racist thinking, the
assumption being that blacks were not individuals but an un-
differentiated group whose fixed station was to be determined
by others. On this question, several possibilities were entertained. There was, first, the idea of black enclaves. Then, there
was the notion of guardianship, involving federal protection
and special laws for the ex-slaves, which might continue for

several years until they were thoroughly prepared for freedom. And, finally, the idea of creating a class of black homesteading landowners was considered. But all three were rejected in favor of a course of action more in accord with the laissez-faire ideas that were predominant at the time.

This approach precluded the possibility of governmental intervention in the natural working of society and the economy either by giving blacks special treatment or by endeavoring to create some form of equality of condition. Instead, the freedmen were to be independent and provide for themselves. This did not, however, mean that the ruthless contemporary dictum of "root, hog, or die" was to become policy, since the federal government intended to do more than simply liberate the slaves and leave them to fend for themselves. Rather, blacks were to be naturalized and armed with the rights enjoyed by U.S. citizens, so that they could defend and expand their freedom. Accordingly, citizenship and legal equality were conferred by the Fourteenth Amendment, while civil rights were bestowed through the Civil Rights Acts of 1866 and 1875.

The suffrage was also a right that accompanied citizenship, but it posed problems since the former slaves were not literate and had not had time to demonstrate their ability to act independently, both of which were traditionally regarded as qualifications for exercising the franchise. In addition, Northerners themselves did not allow blacks to vote. Only six states, with just 5 percent of the section's black population, enfranchised them. Indeed, whenever states held referenda on black suffrage after the war, it was voted down, as Ohio, Minnesota, and Kansas, for example, did in 1867. So hostile were northern whites to Negro suffrage that the Democrats seized on it as the most effective issue to use against their Republican rivals in the postwar years. Thus, by including black suffrage in the Reconstruction Act of 1867, Republicans in Congress were imposing a policy on the South that their own northern constituents would not tolerate for themselves.

Despite the restriction of black suffrage to the South, northern opposition was still tenacious. In the elections held in the North in 1867 soon after the passage of the Reconstruction Act, the Republicans were defeated in Ohio, Pennsylvania, New York, and New Jersey and suffered reduced margins in the New England states. Rather than congratulating them for finally settling Reconstruction, the voters seemed eager to punish them for enfranchising blacks. Because of this, the Republican national convention of 1868 promised not to press black suffrage in the North. At the same time, the party's platform endorsed its imposition on the South. A year later, however, this inconsistent and somewhat hypocritical pledge was broken when Republicans in Congress decided to nationalize black voting rights by constitutional amendment. This risky move was taken because the party's declining electoral prospects could be revived by enfranchising blacks outside the reconstructed states, particularly in Maryland, Missouri, and Tennessee, which contained sizable black populations.

It has been argued, however, that the Republicans' intention in doing this was principled, since they actually lost the votes of angry whites when they enfranchised blacks. In fact, all that this observation proves is that the Republicans miscalculated, since the motive behind an action cannot be deduced from its outcome. Moreover, the framers of the suffrage (15ᵗʰ) amendment were quite aware of the possible negative effect that enfranchising blacks would have on white voters, so they wrote its provisions in highly qualified terms. Therefore, it did not stipulate that suffrage was to be universal but merely that it could not be denied on grounds of race. This timidity allowed for its denial for other reasons, such as illiteracy or lack of property, a loophole that Southerners later exploited in the 1890s. Yet, even with its cautious phrasing, the amendment provoked considerable opposition in the North, and only the appeal to party necessity got it through the legislatures of the Middle Atlantic and Midwestern states. This deep-seated resistance to equal rights meant that federal Reconstruction policy was burdened by an avowed northern hostility to its central premise of black suffrage. /

The enfranchisement of the former slaves was a radical

initiative never even contemplated in the other New World slave societies after Emancipation. It happened in the United States simply because, once the decision was made to reinstitute electoral politics in the South, there was no other source available to provide the basis for a loyal, and therefore Republican, constituency. If the success of Reconstruction and the perpetuation of the party that had saved the nation required that the freedmen, and later all blacks, be given the vote, then it was evidently possible to subordinate racial prejudice. But it entailed a precarious balance of conflicting priorities.

Also precarious were the gains that southern blacks made through the Republicans' program of equal rights. The party offered blacks equality of rights and opportunity. But, of course, the provision of legal rights does not guarantee that they will either be automatically acknowledged by the rest of society or that they will be easily implemented and fulfilled. Pessimism about the outcome was particularly appropriate when the intended beneficiary was a race that most Northerners, Republicans included, believed to be currently, and probably innately, inferior. But the party's provision of equal rights before the law under these circumstances was not malicious or cynical; at most, it was self-deceptive. All the same, the outcome was not difficult to predict, even though Republican congressmen may have wished it to be otherwise.

If Northerners' racial attitudes impeded the successful Reconstruction of the South, so too did their economic interests. The South needed capital to revive its war-torn economy. In addition, it had to build a transportation system and diversify and increase its output in order to catch up with the North. Since the federal government was already engaged in reconstructing the region, the South's congressional delegation arrived in Washington with expectations that aid for economic development would be forthcoming. As one southern Republican congressman, Alfred E. Buck of Alabama, put it: "prosperity to the South aided by a generous policy of internal improvement will more firmly cement and bind us in the family of States" than anything else. To Republicans like Buck, obtaining this aid would also convince southern voters that the new party was in fact a valuable asset to the region.

Despite their importance to the region and the party, the southern Republicans' requests for funds were met with rebuff, not only from the Democrats in Congress, but from their fellow Republicans as well. At the very moment when the South reentered Congress, the supply of subsidies for railroads and waterways began to dry up, as a powerful movement, led by Representative William S. Holman of Indiana, forced the curtailment of a decade-long outpouring of federal largesse, known as the "Great Barbecue." What was left was a dwindling amount of funds for river and harbor improvement which northern congressmen wanted for their own districts and were not about to hand over to representatives from other states, even if more needy. Moreover, they were particularly loath to deny these benefits to their own citizens who had been loyal during the war and give them to rebels instead. Compounding the southern Republicans' difficulties was the rapid turnover in the region's representatives—another unfortunate result of the instability within the party in the South—because it prevented southern congressmen from gaining acceptance, contacts, and seniority in their campaign to extract benefits for their region. As Terry Seip's *The South Returns to Congress* (1983) has shown, the result was that the South, which needed more than the northern states during Reconstruction, actually obtained proportionately less.

On one major subsidy, however, the South did enjoy some success. This was the project for a southern transcontinental railroad to match the Union Pacific route which had just been completed across the North in 1869. A subsidy for a southern line was granted in 1871. Although Southerners had been instrumental in the bill's passage, they were mixed in their reaction to its provisions. Not only was the amount of the subsidy—under twenty million acres of land and no grants of cash or bonds—less than the northern route had received, but there were to be no branch lines to benefit local communities. Furthermore, the gauge was to be northern and the line was to run via St. Louis to Philadelphia and New York rather than to a southeastern terminus. The northern orientation of the route became even more evident after 1872 because Tom Scott of the Pennsylvania Railroad began to take a consuming interest in the project. Southern support accordingly started to wane. This declining enthusiasm was compounded by a growing opposition from established southern railroads that feared the incursions of the Pennsylvania system as well as by increasing suspicion toward railroad rings and government subsidies in general. This was particularly true of the Democrats who, by the mid-1870s, had become a majority of the region's congressional delegation. By this time, Scott's project elicited very little enthusiasm in the South and it died in Congress in 1878, leaving the western end of the route to be built without subsidy by Collis P. Huntington's Southern Pacific.

Yet another way in which Congress could have helped the South economically was by taking measures to compensate for the region's dearth of currency and credit. Because the South had had its own financial arrangements under the Confederacy, it was naturally excluded from the system of national banks and paper money, known as greenbacks, that Washington had instituted during the war in order to expand and regulate the currency. To remedy this severe disadvantage, money had to flow into the South through an increase as well as a redistribution of the existing supply. Southerners, by and large, agreed about this general aim, but the North was divided. The Northeast which had a disproportionate share of the section's national banks and currency supply resisted attempts to inflate and redistribute. Instead, its representatives proposed that the country end its reliance on paper money by returning to specie, that is, silver and gold, as the basis for the currency. This kind of remedy, however, would inevitably contract the amount of currency and increase its value, exactly what the South and most of the Midwest did not want.

The deflationists were not simply a regional interest group; they also had financial orthodoxy on their side when they sought to decrease the volume of greenbacks and peg the money supply to specie. Faced with this, the expansionists had to be content with an increase of a mere $10 million in the Public Credit Act of 1870, a pittance for the beleaguered South. Later, after the panic and depression of 1873 set in, an expansion of the money supply became desperately needed. So a bill was passed which raised the greenback ceiling to $400 million and distributed another $45 million to states with less than their quota. This measure was supported enthusiastically by the midwestern states as well as by the South. Yet, even though it was hardly an extreme proposal, eastern financial interests dubbed it the "inflation bill," and their anxious warnings so convinced President Grant that he vetoed it.

The South reacted to the veto with shock and dismay. The bill's provisions had been barely adequate for a region that, as its leading sponsor, North Carolina's Democratic senator, Augustus Merrimon, complained, was suffering from "a scarcity of money that is hardly endurable." Nevertheless, southern congressmen of both parties had supported it desperately, only to discover that their own region's distress was to be subordinated to economic orthodoxy and northeastern interests. So, in the 1874 elections, the region expressed its displeasure with the Republicans. All the same, Southerners were less punitive than were the Midwesterners, since the latter's vote against the Republicans gave control of the House to their Democratic rivals. But it was clear that the North as a whole was unsympathetic to the South's economic plight. Moreover, the Republicans of the Northeast had shown unmistakably that they had no intention of abandoning their own interests to help their vulnerable southern colleagues. Perhaps it was unreasonable to expect that they would, but the result was that the southern Republicans were left unable to vindicate their claim to be indispensable to the region's future prosperity.

Economic help from the North was still possible from the private sector, and Southerners sought it avidly. But, once again, they were to discover that the interests of Northerners were not compatible with those of the South. No amount of pleading that the devastated and less developed region needed preferential treatment could persuade outside entrepreneurs to do the South's bidding. Northern railroad promoters wanted to invest in the South—and they did—but their interest was in building trunk routes, not local lines. Furthermore, rather than laying new track, they preferred to consolidate existing roads into systems linked with their northern networks. Since consolidation was almost certain to result in control, Southerners feared that their encouragement of large corporate mergers would place southern roads in the hands of outsiders with monopolistic ambitions. As examples, they could point to Tom Scott's Southern Railway Security Company, which, by 1873, was operating thirteen lines and 2,000 miles of track, or to Charles Morgan's extensive schemes in Texas and Louisiana.

To prevent this from happening, state legislatures refused to issue charters or appropriate funds. They also attempted to exert control over the roads by insisting that state bonds and endorsements as well as private subscriptions constitute a majority of the financing. In this way, local needs and concerns could be met. But the trouble was that there was insufficient cash available for private contributions, while the Republican state governments themselves were so precarious and unreliable that their securities depreciated and their backing became a liability. After all, there was little incentive to invest in a state like Florida, for example, where the leading Democratic newspaper once avowed: "Our only hope lies in the state's utter financial bankruptcy; and Heaven grant that it may speedily come." When, with help from the Democrats, state finances began to founder in the early 1870s, northern railroad investment as well as southern control over it were both severely curtailed.

The divergence of interest between outside investors and the South was also evident in the cotton industry. After the war, many Southerners wanted to develop a textile manufacturing industry of their own, in order to diversify their economy and end their dependence as producers of raw cotton on buyers in the North who then turned it into finished goods.

An added incentive for domestic manufacture was provided by the wartime federal tax on cotton that was shipped outside the South, because southern growers could avoid the onerous levy by converting the cotton into cloth themselves. In their campaign for cotton mills, Southerners might have expected capital investment from Northerners who had an eye for personal profit and wanted to encourage the South's economic revival. In fact, however, Northerners wanted the South to recuperate so as to provide a market for their own food and finished goods; they did not want it to revive and become a rival manufacturer.

In the debate over the repeal of the cotton tax in 1866, northern congressmen were quite unabashed in expressing their desire that, as Senator Thomas Hendricks of Indiana said, "the southern states [continue to] furnish the natural market to the Northwest for their great productions." The Northerners anticipated that removal of the tax would keep cotton prices down and also encourage planters to continue growing the raw cotton that the northern mills needed. If Southerners remained cotton producers rather than manufacturers, a potentially dangerous competitor, with ready access to cheap labor and raw materials, would be eliminated. So the levy was repealed in February 1868. Furthermore, when northern textile interests did invest in the postwar South, it was for the purpose of encouraging the growing of cotton, not its manufacture. This self-interested combativeness was not confined to the North, however, since the South's avowed aim in wanting to produce its own cotton textiles was to gain economic self-determination and end Yankee dominance. Cotton was therefore an economic battleground between North and South, not an arena for cooperation. As in other areas of economic policy, the South was, therefore, merely one of several regional interests competing for advantage. Consequently, there would be no Marshall Plan or preferential treatment for the former rebels, even though they needed aid and even though their congressmen were Republicans.

Although it is difficult to tell, there might conceivably have been more sympathy for, and greater involvement in, the reconstructed South if the radicals had been able to maintain their influence within the Republican party beyond the immediate postwar years. After all, they were the ones most determined to abolish slavery, grant blacks equal rights, and democratize and transform southern society. And they perhaps would have insisted that this initiative be sustained and not allowed to falter. But, by about 1870, radicalism was in eclipse and the Republican party was assuming a more conservative, less energetic temper.

The radicals conceived of government as an active force responsible for removing all barriers to individual advancement and opportunity. In this way, government was to help achieve the harmonious society of equals that was their goal. Toward the realization of this aim, the abolition of chattel slavery and the granting of equal rights were essential. But this initiative was just part of a continuing and expanding agenda of reform. In the northern states after the war, radicals were active in pressing government to take responsibility for social welfare by passing public health legislation, setting standards for tenement housing, providing free education, and funding hospitals and asylums. In New York and Massachusetts in particular, there was a spate of successful reform introduced by the radicals in the late 1860s. Their concern that government guarantee equal rights also drew the radicals into the emerging movements to end unequal treatment of women and workingmen. Led by Susan B. Anthony and Elizabeth Cady Stanton who had earlier been active abolitionists, women began to demand the suffrage. Meanwhile, labor reformers and trade unionists rallied behind the demand for the eight-hour day. These campaigns against gender slavery and wage slavery were both a natural outgrowth of the abolition of chattel slavery as well as a logical extension of the radicals' commitment to equal rights.

The attainment of equal rights was expected to produce harmony in society, but the practical attempt to win them engendered political conflict. Women's demand for the vote coincided with the Republicans' campaign for black suffrage in 1869 and 1870. Neither of these proposals was popular and so the party refused to jeopardize passage of the Fifteenth Amendment by simultaneously identifying itself with the vote for women. Accordingly, Republicans disassociated themselves from the suffragists, forcing Anthony and Stanton to rebuke them by taking their cause to the Democrats. Rebuffed there, they soon decided to abandon politics altogether and agitate the issue independently. A similar outcome occurred with the labor question. Although intended to give workers a measure of equality and thus balance and harmonize relations between labor and capital, legislation reducing the hours of work infringed both the law of contract as well as the employer's claim to be able to set the terms of employment. As a result, manufacturers opposed it so vehemently that the party concluded that the issue was too divisive and politically damaging to pursue further. By the mid-1870s, workingmen's organizations also began to give up on politics, deciding, like the feminists, to wage their struggle on their own.

The effect of this decision on the Republican party itself was also far-reaching. By curtailing, if not abandoning, its crusade for equal rights and reform, the party had rejected the possibility of broadening its constituency by drawing in women, workers, and other excluded and disadvantaged groups. Also, advocacy of equal rights did not seem to produce harmony. Rather, it generated rivalries, with the risk that the party might lose more support than it gained. And, finally, pursuit of the radicals' agenda was certain to keep the party in constant turmoil, since it required the Republicans to continually espouse causes and agitate issues. As E. L. Godkin, the editor of *The Nation* and a one-time radical, began to see it, there seemed to be no end to the activism and responsibilities of the state as conceived by the radicals; so limits had to be set. "The government must get out of the 'protective' business and the 'subsidy' business and the 'improvement' and 'development' business," he concluded. Rather than seeking new issues and taking on new responsibilities, government should identify existing legitimate interests and try simply to adjudicate the differences between them, thereby functioning as an arbitrator rather than a champion. In effect, government and the Republican party needed restraint and repose after a decade of activism.

This shift in the mood of northern Republicanism amounted to a recognition of two postwar realities. The first of these concerned the very nature and identity of the party itself now that the emotive issues of slavery and the war, which had had such a shaping influence on it during the previous decade, were settled. This outcome presented the organization with a critical decision. Either it could change direction and develop new questions and new constituencies, or else it could try to stay with its past record and its existing support. The radicals naturally identified with the first of the two scenarios, since they believed that issues and ideology were the essence of Republicanism. Unfortunately for them, however, the kinds of concerns that were arising after the war seemed likely, as Godkin pointed out, to destabilize, even endanger, the party. So the Republicans began to turn increasingly to the other alternative—reliance on their current support and identity. As this occurred, the ability of the party to function efficiently and mobilize its cadre of known adherents became essential to its electoral success, since it could not expect to gain additional support from new, non-Republican constituencies. The result was that politicians who were skillful managers and loyal party operatives assumed increasing importance and so, predictably, they rose to positions of influence. In effect, the identity of the party and the meaning it had for its supporters began to take precedence over the formulation of issues and the expansion of the party's electoral base.

As the party's tone and image altered in these ways, so too did its attitude toward Reconstruction. Rather than being viewed as a continuing commitment to reorder the South, Reconstruction came to be regarded as a matter that was completed and settled by the region's readmission to Congress and the passage of the Fifteenth Amendment. As such, it was no longer an issue. Instead, it was merely a past achievement and an aspect of Republicanism's identity as the party that had saved the Union. To maintain this identity in the voters' minds, the party had to sustain the Reconstruction governments it had set up in the South and to constantly reaffirm its pledge to keep the ex-Confederates from thwarting the will and authority of the victorious North, as embodied in the Republican party. But no further involvement was required beyond the maintenance and enforcement of its past policy.

The other reality confronting northern Republicans was the failure of their notion of "free labor." In the 1850s, the Republicans had not simply opposed slavery, they had offered an alternative vision of a society in which laborers were free. In a society based on free labor, workers were not condemned to the status of wage-earner but could rise in their lifetime to become economically independent and even able to hire laborers of their own. As Lincoln, citing his own rise as proof, stated it: "There is no permanent class of hired laborers amongst us [in the nonslaveholding states]. Twenty five years ago, I was a hired laborer. The hired laborer of yesterday, labors on his own account to-day; and will hire others to labor for him to-morrow. Advancement—improvement in condition—is the order of things in a society of equals." In a social system like that of the North which was thought to be open and fluid, there were no barriers to prevent independent producers, whether urban artisans or rural farmworkers, from eventually becoming employers and owners themselves. There were, therefore, neither permanent classes nor an unremitting class conflict in Republican America.

What was wrong with the South, in the eyes of the Republicans, was that its system of dependent slave labor and its depreciation of the value of work made it impossible for anything like free labor to flourish. With the ending of slavery, therefore, the introduction of free labor was now possible. Then, the emancipated slaves as well as the numerous dependent downtrodden whites could themselves anticipate economic advancement and autonomy. Yet, when the opportunity to effect these changes arose after the war, the Republicans paid virtually no attention to the "poor whites," while the freedmen were allowed to lapse into the dependency of sharecropping. Even Lincoln himself had sanctioned a system of contract labor in Louisiana that kept blacks working in gangs on fixed wages, a scheme that obviously precluded the mobility and independence so essential for free labor. A variant of the contract system was then continued by the Freedmen's Bureau. Even though bureau agents acknowledged that this was only a temporary, transitional phase, their rigid maintenance of an unbreakable year-long contract still deprived the laborer of mobility and bargaining power, once the terms had been set.

After the bureau withdrew, the annual contract was continued, along with its provision that payment for rent and labor be made in shares of the future crop rather than in cash. Indeed, the contract lay at the heart of the system of tenancy and sharecropping that became universal throughout the agricultural South. Under this arrangement, whatever independence the laborer had anticipated from his farming on shares without close supervision began to evaporate as the crop lien and constant indebtedness tied him down and denied him all hope of advancement. With the further tightening of the landlord's control in the legislation of the mid-1870s that accompanied Redemption, the laborer was reduced to a status akin to slavery. As a number of historians, especially Eric Foner, in his *Nothing But Freedom: Emancipation and Its Legacy* (1983), have been making increasingly apparent, this condition fell far short of the concept of free labor touted by the northern Republicans. In fact, there was some recognition, even at the time, of what the system was like and what its emergence portended. In February 1875, Alabama's Republican legislators pointed out its implications in a worried memorial they sent to President Grant. "The issue [of the war]," they said, "was free-labor institutions and principles against slave-labor institutions and principles." Yet "the drift and tendency of all of [this legislation] is to establish a system of compulsory labor and peonage utterly inconsistent with the genius and spirit of free-labor States and institutions." Evidently, labor after slavery was to be coerced and dependent rather than "free."

Free labor was not suppressed in the South alone, however. It also failed to emerge in the North, despite the Republicans' assumption that it was the norm. After the war, the factory system proliferated and it was accompanied by the development of a large unskilled and routinized work force. As a result, the likelihood of workers improving their prospects and rising to become self-employed diminished rapidly. Rather than being independent producers, workers were falling into the permanent condition and status of a proletariat. Forced to recognize their declining position, they began to organize collectively into trade unions and saw themselves engaged in a continuous struggle with capital. Thus, the existence of "wage slavery," which Republicans had dismissed earlier as an aberration that "free labor" would automatically eliminate, was actually becoming widespread. In fact, by the 1870s, the notion of free labor seemed to be an anachronism, an ideal that was quite possibly out-of-date in the 1850s but that, twenty years later, appeared completely irrelevant. And if proof were needed that free labor was nothing more than an ideal, it was dramatically provided by the labor unrest of the mid-1870s that culminated in the violent nationwide railroad strike of 1877. Northern society, like that of the South, was evidently not a harmony of interests but was quite possibly a hierarchy of classes.

While the organizational structure as well as the ideology of the Republican party were undergoing significant alteration, its relationship with its southern branch remained unchanged. Throughout Reconstruction, the connection between the northern Republicans and the party they had created in the South continued to be based on dependence and subordination. This reliance could have resulted in the North's taking on the responsibility for nurturing its vulnerable offspring in order to ensure that it survived and grew. But that did not happen. Rather, the reverse occurred, for the southern party was virtually left to fend for itself, as Richard H. Abbott's *The*

Republican Party and the South, 1855–1877 (1986) has shown. For instance, it was given almost no political help. The Republican national executive committee was grudgingly parsimonious in its provision of funds for party building and campaign financing. Also, with the exception of a brief flurry of activity in North Carolina in 1872, no prominent northern Republican ventured south after 1868 to lend his prestige and aid at election time. Even Senator Henry Wilson of Massachusetts and Representative William D. "Pig Iron" Kelley who had gone down in 1867 and 1868 never toured the South again. And finally, Republicans in Congress did little, if anything, to help their southern counterparts by responding to their pleas for economic assistance and sympathetic financial legislation. Instead, they sent them home to face the voters empty handed.

This indifference about the fate of the southern party they had so agonizingly created was puzzling, to say the least. It arose from what was perhaps the central dilemma of Reconstruction. After the war, the hegemony of the Republican party, possibly even its survival, was contingent upon its ability to reconstruct the South in such a way as to prevent its returning to Congress with a delegation that was solidly Democratic. This was the Republicans' hidden agenda from 1864 to 1868. But once that dangerous outcome had been forestalled by the readmission of a Republican South, there was no vital need for further political involvement there. Northern Republicans could now focus their attention on reassessing their political priorities and reorganizing their party apparatus so as to be able to maintain and then strengthen their hold on the North. If they could do this successfully, they would keep control of Congress and the presidency without having to rely on the South. Of course, this would be easier to do if the South remained largely Republican, but it might not be necessary. Thus, whatever happened to the southern Republican party after 1868 had to be evaluated, not so much in terms of its impact on the South itself, but of how it contributed to the health of the party in its northern stronghold.

The fundamental assumption of Republican policy was

that the party was, after all, northern in origin and character. So the extent of its involvement in the South was determined by how its actions there were perceived by the northern electorate. This, however, required a delicate balancing act. On the one hand, it would be politically disastrous in the North to let the southern regimes, and therefore the whole Reconstruction policy, collapse without a fight. On the other hand, a continuous and deepening entanglement in southern affairs in order to save those governments was also likely to be damaging. Therefore, there were strict limits to what the party could and would do to keep the South Republican.

The restrictions on Republican policy in the South were revealed in the controversy over the Force Acts of 1870–71. In response to the outbreak of Klan violence and the effort to interfere with the right of Republicans, mainly blacks, to vote, the party introduced into Congress two pieces of legislation to increase the federal government's ability to put down lawlessness and protect voting rights. This expansion of federal involvement was thought to be justified, not so much because blacks needed protection but as a reaction to what were increasingly being referred to as "southern outrages." Federal intervention could be supported if it were viewed as a necessary extension of the war, begun in 1860, against southern subversion of federal authority and legitimate government. "Waving the bloody shirt" in this way resonated with the constituency that the party had built up around its armed struggle to save the Union. But if the government's actions were seen as going beyond this preventative aim, the voters would resist, as they did two years later when an expanded civil rights bill was proposed.

By the mid-1870s, however, even the limited appeal of the "bloody shirt" and "southern outrages" was insufficient to warrant the sending of troops to save the faltering southern regimes. Their maintenance seemed increasingly to require an unending military presence. This was too absorbing and far-reaching to be tolerated, and so it began to be politically counterproductive in the North. Although Grant did intervene in

Louisiana's politics early in 1875, a request for troops in Mississippi in the summer of that year became an issue in the upcoming northern elections. Feeling he had to choose between losing Mississippi or losing Ohio, Grant opted, as expected, to let the southern state go by refusing to heed Governor Ames's desperate plea.

This trend culminated in the Compromise of 1877 that arose out of the disputed 1876 presidential election. The Compromise proved to be the most obvious as well as the final indication that the interests of southern Republicanism were subsidiary. By means of this celebrated negotiation, the last three Reconstruction governments—in South Carolina, Florida, and Louisiana—were sacrificed in return for their vote in the electoral college for the Republican presidential candidate, Rutherford B. Hayes. By contrast with 1867, the party's control of the presidency and its continuing competitiveness in Congress and the northern states seemed no longer dependent on keeping the South out of Democratic hands. The situation was now reversed, in fact. The South was to be surrendered in order, ironically, to keep the North out of Democratic hands.

Conclusion

The refusal of Northerners to continue their support of the beleaguered and collapsing Reconstruction governments was really quite understandable. After all, the amount of intervention that was needed to sustain them did appear to be boundless. This was, in fact, a persistent feature of Reconstruction. Nothing ever was enough; more action, it seemed, was always needed. At the outset, the slaves had been emancipated and the rebellion subdued, but these considerable achievements soon proved to be insufficient. Subsequently, the slaves were then enfranchised and the South reorganized politically, with the formation of a new party and the creation of new governments. Even this was not enough, since these Reconstruction governments constantly called on the North for further aid and protection.

Because it was always falling short, Reconstruction has been judged harshly as a failure. Critics have argued that much more should have been done when Washington had the South, helpless and defeated, in its hands. Land should have been confiscated and redistributed to the freedmen. The rebellious South should have been treated as a conquered province and kept under military occupation until significant changes had occurred in the attitudes and behavior of its population. But, wise though these proposals may have been, they were not acceptable and feasible at the time. And it is neither fair nor good history to blame the protagonists for not doing more.

In fact, Reconstruction's ultimate lack of success is not attributable solely to its having been insufficiently radical and far-reaching in conception. Rather, the difficulties it encountered arose because the policy was internally contradictory. For it was both radical, yet not radical enough. The intent of the policy was to restore self-government to the South through the creation of fully functioning elected governments. Once this was accomplished by 1868, the Union was considered restored. This meant that federal-state relations were again operative; the civil authorities were once more supreme over the military, which in turn was soon to be removed from the South altogether; and, finally, a self-sustaining electoral system, consisting of two competitive parties, was reintroduced into the southern states. Thus, customary procedures had been reestablished and the aberrations of the postwar era had been finally removed. Paradoxically, the means employed to achieve these familiar and normal goals were in fact novel and quite radical. The slaves had not just been emancipated and endowed with citizenship, but they had also obtained equality before the law and even the vote. Indeed, they now held office and constituted the overwhelming majority of Republican voters in the South. Furthermore, the South's new governments had been chosen by electorates that had been screened and manipulated by Washington so as to produce a prearranged result. And then, finally, the entire scheme was carried out under military supervision.

For most mid-nineteenth-century Americans, this anomalous process was certainly a radical departure from traditional practices. For Southerners, in particular, it was unacceptably extreme. Yet the Republican party and the governments it now ran were expected to function and be accepted within the reconstructed South's political system as if normal circumstances prevailed.

Caught in this contradiction between the means employed and the goals sought after, the Republicans in the South as well as the federal authorities in Washington were continually forced to adopt extraordinary measures, while claiming at the same time that nothing unusual was involved or intended. By the mid-1870s, this discrepancy had become too glaring to sustain. Continual intervention and ever more radical steps seemed to be essential to the preservation of governments whose intended purpose had been to make these very same actions unnecessary.

This contradiction at the heart of federal Reconstruction policy meant that it was caught in an impossible dilemma that would deprive it of success. Thus, the reasons for the disappointing outcome of Reconstruction are not at all straightforward. Like Janus, the policy presented two contrasting faces, and therein lies the riddle of Reconstruction that has so puzzled and frustrated historians ever since.

BIBLIOGRAPHICAL ESSAY

The historical literature on the era of Emancipation and Reconstruction can be best approached through several influential historiographical essays. Among the most important are Howard K. Beale, "On Rewriting Reconstruction History," *American Historical Review* (1940); Bernard Weisberger, "The Dark and Bloody Ground of Reconstruction Historiography," *Journal of Southern History* (1959); and Herman Belz, "The New Orthodoxy in Reconstruction Historiography," *Reviews in American History* (1973). Two more recent essays have suggested that a turning point, or watershed, in the way historians have treated the period has now been reached. John Hope Franklin's presidential address, "Mirror for Americans: A Century of Reconstruction History," *American Historical Review* (1980), suggested that, by the end of the 1970s, the passion and moralizing that had previously permeated historical writing on the era were finally dissipating. A few years later, Eric Foner's "Reconstruction Revisited," *Reviews in American History* (1982) took issue with the post-Revisionists' emphasis on the continuity and conservatism of Reconstruction and proposed that historians henceforth acknowledge both the amount of change that actually occurred during Reconstruction and the importance of the role that class played in the reconstructed South.

The historiography of the Reconstruction period has gone

through three phases. The first of these was established by the New South school in the early twentieth century. Usually, it was referred to as the Dunning school after William A. Dunning of Columbia University, who trained many of the young historians whose studies of the period contributed to the emerging interpretation. Dunning himself was far more measured and dispassionate than his students and his *Essays on the Civil War and Reconstruction* (1897) and *Reconstruction, Political and Economic, 1865–1877* (1907) are thorough and still valuable examinations of the era. The output of the school generally consisted of a number of studies of individual states during Reconstruction, the most influential of which were J. G. de Roulhac Hamilton's *Reconstruction in North Carolina* (1914); C. Mildred Thompson's *Reconstruction in Georgia* (1915); Walter L. Fleming's *Civil War and Reconstruction in Alabama* (1905); James W. Garner's *Reconstruction in Mississippi* (1901); and Charles Ramsdell's *Reconstruction in Texas* (1910). Although conforming to the most advanced methods of scholarship at the time, these works, mainly by Southerners who grew up in the post-Reconstruction decades, were sharply critical of Reconstruction because it was needlessly punitive and extreme towards the South. This aversion to the period was subsequently etched into the American public consciousness by two widely read books—Claude Bowers's *The Tragic Era* (1929) and George F. Milton's *The Age of Hate* (1930)— and by two of the most popular movies of the twentieth century—D. W. Griffith's *Birth of a Nation* (1915) and *Gone With The Wind* (1940).

While the New South orthodoxy was becoming firmly established in the first half of the century, a number of historians were challenging it, though to little avail. As early as 1910, W. E. B. DuBois published a little-noticed article, "Reconstruction and Its Benefits," in the *American Historical Review*. Then, in 1935, he produced a full-length study, entitled *Black Reconstruction in America, 1860–1880*. DuBois, who was in fact the first Revisionist, emphasized the role of blacks in Reconstruction and characterized the period as one of class struggle. His

Marxist approach was taken up by James S. Allen in his *Reconstruction: The Battle for Democracy, 1865–1876* (1937), while Roger Shugg's *Origins of Class-struggle in Louisiana* (1939) reiterated the centrality of class conflict. Concurrently, DuBois's focus on blacks was being developed by Alrutheus A. Taylor in three state studies of the Negro in South Carolina (1924), in Virginia (1926), and in Tennessee (1938) as well as by Horace Mann Bond in his *Negro Education in Alabama: A Study in Cotton and Steel* (1939), which also drew attention to the importance of economics in Reconstruction. Also Revisionist in tone was Francis B. Simkins and Robert H.Woody's *South Carolina During Reconstruction* (1932).

It was not until the 1950s and 1960s that an alternative view of Reconstruction made headway against the New South interpretation. With the emergence of the civil rights movement and what was known as the Second Reconstruction of the South, a climate of opinion arose that made the prevailing viewpoint untenable. The acceptance of the Revisionist approach was signalled by the publication in the early 1960s of two influential surveys of the period written in the new mold—John Hope Franklin's *Reconstruction: After the Civil War* (1961) and Kenneth Stampp's *The Era of Reconstruction, 1865–1877* (1965). The Revisionists virtually turned the prevailing orthodoxy upside-down by arguing that the Republicans' southern policies were not vindictive but progressive and realistic, while Johnson and the South were reactionary and obstructionist. Reconstruction's failure was attributable therefore to the intensity of the opposition it encountered, not primarily to shortcomings of its own.

The Revisionists' reinterpretation focussed on two central features of the history of the period. The first was the contest between President Johnson and Congress over the formulation of federal policy for the defeated South. The major works were Eric McKitrick's *Andrew Johnson and Reconstruction* (1960); John and LaWanda Cox's *Politics, Principle, and Prejudice, 1865–1866: Dilemma of Reconstruction America* (1963); and William R. Brock's *An American Crisis: Congress and Recon-*

struction, 1865–1867 (1963). All three found Johnson's approach to be inflexible and conservative and blamed him for the political crisis in Washington. By contrast, most Revisionists were sympathetic to the difficulties faced by the congressional Republicans. The latter, they found, were activated by principle rather than by self-interest and partisanship. Hans Trefousse's 1969 study of *The Radical Republicans* was subtitled *Lincoln's Vanguard for Racial Justice*, while John and LaWanda Cox claimed that principle, not party advantage, dictated their decision to introduce the Fifteenth Amendment ("Negro Suffrage and Reconstruction Politics: The Problem of Motivation in Reconstruction Historiography," *Journal of Southern History* [1967]). Meanwhile, the continuing vitality of the abolitionists and their contacts with the Republican party were pointed out by James McPherson, in his *The Struggle for Equality: Abolitionists and the Negro in the Civil War and Reconstruction* (1964).

This reassessment of Republican intentions coincided with a parallel trend among economic historians to reject Howard K. Beale's view, in *The Critical Year: A Study of Andrew Johnson and Reconstruction* (1930), that their southern policy was motivated primarily by economic interests. Robert Sharkey's *Money, Class and Party: An Economic Study of the Civil War and Reconstruction* (1950); Irwin Unger's *The Greenback Era* (1964); and Stanley Coben's "Northeastern Businessmen and Radical Reconstruction," *Mississippi Valley Historical Review* (1959) showed that the Republicans were so divided on economic policy that it could not have been a primary consideration. In similar fashion, Joseph B. James's *The Framing of the Fourteenth Amendment* (1956) refuted the widely accepted assumption that protection of corporations rather than individuals had been the party's hidden but real intention in the amendment's civil rights provisions.

The Revisionists also produced sympathetic biographies of leading Republicans, namely Fawn Brodie's *Thaddeus Stevens: Scourge of the South* (1959); Hans Trefousse's *Benjamin F. Wade: Radical Republican of Ohio* (1963); Benjamin P.

Thomas and Harold M. Hyman's *Stanton: The Life and Times of Lincoln's Secretary of War* (1962); and David Donald's rather more critical *Charles Sumner and the Rights of Man* (1970), the second volume of his life of the Massachusetts radical. David Donald also examined Republican voting behavior in Congress in his *The Politics of Reconstruction, 1863–1867* (1965) and Herman Belz analyzed the party's wartime discussion of Reconstruction policies in *Reconstructing the Union* (1969), both of which refuted T. Harry Williams's earlier view, in his *Lincoln and the Radicals* (1942), that the Republican party was a monolith.

The other area of Revisionist concern was their reexamination of the course of Reconstruction in the South. The major achievement here was their discovery that, contrary to the assumptions of the New South school, blacks had played an active role, despite the vigorous opposition of southern whites. Martin Abbott's *The Freedmen's Bureau in South Carolina, 1865–1872* (1967) built on George Bentley's previous *A History of the Freedmen's Bureau* (1955), while William McFeely's *Yankee Stepfather* (1968) and John A. Carpenter's *Sword and Olive Branch* (1964) were biographies of Oliver Otis Howard, the bureau commissioner. The educational and land-reform experiment on the Sea Islands was described by Willie Lee Rose's *Rehearsal for Reconstruction: The Port Royal Experiment* (1964), while Joel Williamson's *After Slavery: The Negro in South Carolina during Reconstruction, 1861–1877* (1965); Joe Richardson's *The Negro in the Reconstruction of Florida, 1865–1877* (1965); and Vernon Wharton's *The Negro in Mississippi, 1865–1890* (1947) assessed the black experience in three states. Okon E. Uya's *From Slavery to Public Service: Robert Smalls, 1839–1915* (1971); Victor Ullman's *Martin Delaney* (1971); and Peggy Lamson's *The Glorious Failure: Robert Brown Elliot and Reconstruction in South Carolina* (1973) presented full portraits of three leading black politicians in South Carolina whose lives and contribution were only dimly known before. And these were followed by Loren Schweninger's *James T. Rapier and Reconstruction* (1973) and Peter D.

Klingman's *Josiah Walls: Florida's Black Congressman in Reconstruction* (1976).

Revisionists also rehabilitated the reputation of the new Republican party in the South. The identity of the native whites who affiliated with it was reexamined in David Donald's "The Scalawag in Mississippi Reconstruction," *Journal of Southern History* (1944); Warren Ellem's "Who were the Mississippi Scalawags?" *Journal of Southern History* (1972); Allen Trelease's "Who were the Scalawags?" *Journal of Southern History* (1963); Otto Olsen's "Reconsidering the Scalawags," *Civil War History* (1966); and Sarah Wiggins's *The Scalawag in Alabama Politics, 1865–1881* (1977). Also relevant to this discussion is Thomas B. Alexander's "Persistent Whiggery in the Confederate South," *Journal of Southern History* (1961). The party's northern membership was reexamined in Richard Current's "Carpetbaggers Reconsidered," in *A Festschrift for Frederick B. Artz* (1964); in Otto Olsen's biography of a leading North Carolina carpetbagger, Albion Tourgée, entitled *Carpetbagger's Crusade* (1965); and in Richard L. Hume's article on the southern constitutional conventions of 1868, "Carpetbaggers in the Reconstruction South," *Journal of American History* (1977). William McKee Evans examined the Republicans' performance at the local level in his *Ballots and Fence Rails: Reconstruction on the Lower Cape Fear* (1967).

The Revisionists' frontal challenge to the New South school had reversed previous assumptions and judgments, the upshot of which was the rehabilitation of the Republicans, both in Congress and in the South, along with their allies, the blacks. With this accomplished, historians in the 1970s and after began to go beyond the categories and preoccupations of the Revisionists to examine systematically and in some detail how Reconstruction was conceived and implemented as well as to open up new areas for investigation, chiefly those that were economic and social rather than political in nature. The result has been that, during the last decade, historians have become more critical of the Republicans than the Revisionists had been, while the period itself has been evaluated more on the basis of its disappointing long-term outcome than on its short-term opportunities and gains. By and large, therefore, post-Revisionist historiography has stressed the relative conservatism and continuity of the Reconstruction era.

In the first place, the role of the Republicans in Washington in creating and enforcing southern policy has been viewed more critically. Les Benedict's *A Compromise of Principle: Congressional Republicans and Reconstruction, 1863–1869* (1974) pointed out that the radicals in the party had little influence over the shape of Reconstruction policy. According to William Gillette's *Retreat from Reconstruction, 1869–1879* (1979), which analyzed presidential enforcement of Reconstruction, this conservative thrust was maintained once the policy went into operation. The calculations and goals of the South in its attempt to elude Reconstruction were explained in Michael Perman's *Reunion Without Compromise: The South and Reconstruction, 1865–1868* (1973), which, in the process, revealed the shortcomings of federal policies based on consent. Terry Seip's *The South Returns to Congress: Men, Economic Measures, and Intersectional Relationships, 1868–1879* (1983) showed how unsupportive northern Republicans were of their southern colleagues. Richard Abbott's *The Republican Party and the South, 1855–1877* (1986) revealed how limited was the concern of northern Republicans to build an enduring base for their party in the South. And, finally, the conservatism of Republican constitutionalism was depicted in Harold Hyman's *A More Perfect Union* (1975) and in Les Benedict's "Preserving the Constitution: The Conservative Basis of Radical Reconstruction," *Journal of American History* (1974). Despite their general caution, the Republicans did take the radical step of impeaching the president. In his *The Impeachment and Trial of Andrew Johnson* (1973), Les Benedict supported their action as politically necessary, thereby countering the hostile assessment in David M. DeWitt's earlier book with the same title, published in 1903. Hans Trefousse's *Impeachment of a President* (1975) also revised and updated DeWitt's approach.

The Republican party's record in the South was also treated

more critically. While acknowledging the party's dilemma and the power of the white opposition, historians now drew attention to the Republicans' own internal shortcomings. Elizabeth S. Nathans's earlier *Losing the Peace: Georgia Republicans and Reconstruction, 1865–1871* (1968) was supplemented by Carl Moneyhon's *Republicanism in Reconstruction Texas* (1980); William C. Harris's *The Day of the Carpetbagger: Republican Reconstruction in Mississippi* (1979); Jerrell H. Shofner's *Nor Is It Over Yet* (1974) on Florida Reconstruction; Joe Gray Taylor's *Louisiana Reconstructed, 1863–1877* (1974); and Ted Tunnell's *Crucible of Reconstruction: War, Radicalism and Race in Louisiana, 1862–1877* (1984). The Republicans' divisive factionalism was the focus of Otto Olsen's edited collection of essays on six states, *Reconstruction and Redemption in the South* (1980), while Mark Summers's *Railroads, Reconstruction and the Gospel of Prosperity: Aid under the Radical Republicans, 1865–1877* (1984) recounted the party's mismanagement of its crucial railroad policy. Mills Thornton's essay, "Fiscal Policy and the Failure of Radical Reconstruction in the Lower South," pointed out the political liabilities in Republican tax measures, and Lawrence Powell's article on "The Politics of Livelihood: Carpetbaggers in the Deep South" suggested that Northerners were motivated more by the need for place and patronage than by principle. Both essays appeared in Morgan Kousser and James McPherson, editors, *Region, Race and Reconstruction: Essays in Honor of C. Vann Woodward* (1982).

In the 1970s, blacks' experience of Emancipation and Reconstruction received an immense amount of attention from historians. The immediate response to Emancipation was assessed in Leon Litwack's *Been in the Storm So Long: The Aftermath of Slavery* (1979). Louis Gerteis's *From Contraband to Freedman* (1973) was critical of federal labor policy, while Donald Nieman's *To Set the Law in Motion* (1979) described the shortcomings in the Freedmen's Bureau's legal and labor provisions. More approving was Herman Belz's analysis of federal civil rights legislation, *A New Birth of Freedom* (1976) and his broader study, *Emancipation and Equal Rights* (1978). Louisiana, which was the focus of so much attention prior to and after Emancipation, has been treated by Peter Ripley's *Slaves and Freedmen in Civil War Louisiana* (1976); Peyton McCrary's *Abraham Lincoln and Reconstruction: The Louisiana Experiment* (1978); and LaWanda Cox's *Lincoln and Black Freedom* (1981).

The freedmen's search for land was described in Edward Magdol's *A Right to the Land: Essays on the Freedmen's Community* (1977); Carol Bleser's *The Promised Land: The History of the South Carolina Land Commission* (1969); Elizabeth Bethel's *Promiseland* (1981); Janet Sharp Hermann's study of the Davis Bend experiment in Mississippi, *The Pursuit of a Dream* (1981); and Claude F. Oubre's *Forty Acres and a Mule* (1978). The provision of education for the freedmen has been examined in Robert Morris, *Reading, 'Riting and Reconstruction* (1981); Jacqueline Jones, *Soldiers of Light and Love* (1980); and Ronald Butchart, *Northern Schools, Southern Blacks and Reconstruction* (1980). The question of separate schools was addressed by William P. Vaughn's *Schools for All* (1974), while the nature of racial separation during and after Reconstruction was delineated in Howard Rabinowitz's *Race Relations in the Urban South, 1865–1890* (1978), which challenged C. Vann Woodward's *The Strange Career of Jim Crow* (1955). Vann Woodward's stimulating comparative essay on Emancipation and Reconstruction, "The Price of Freedom," appeared in *What Was Freedom's Price?* edited by David Sansing (1978).

The role of black politicians received increasing attention with the appearance of more biographies as well as case studies like Charles Vincent's *Black Legislators in Louisiana during Reconstruction* (1976) and Thomas Holt's *Black Over White: Negro Political Leadership in South Carolina during Reconstruction* (1977). Holt and Armstead Robinson, in his "Beyond the Realm of Social Consensus: New Meanings of Reconstruction for American History," *Journal of American History* (1981), both stressed the political liabilities of the social divisions among blacks. Meanwhile, the collection of essays on

Southern Black Leaders of the Reconstruction Era (1982), edited by Howard Rabinowitz, focussed on how blacks functioned and operated in Reconstruction politics.

The status of blacks in Reconstruction had an economic
as well as political dimension, and so historians turned their
attention to the nature of the system of land and labor in the
post-Emancipation South. For the most part, they found the
agricultural economy and the position of black laborers within
it not all that different from the situation under slavery. The
persistence of existing attitudes and practices on the plantation
were indicated in James Roark's *Masters Without Slaves:
Southern Planters in the Civil War and Reconstruction* (1977)
and Lawrence Powell's *New Masters: Northern Planters during
the Civil War and Reconstruction* (1980) as well as in Jonathan
Wiener's *Social Origins of the New South: Alabama, 1860–
1885* (1978) and Michael Wayne's *The Reshaping of Plantation
Society: The Natchez District, 1860–1880* (1983), the latter two
works showing that planters succeeded in keeping possession
of their lands and maintaining their economic dominance.
Wiener and Dwight B. Billings, Jr., in his *Planters and the
Making of a 'New South'* (1979), argued that the planter class
also managed to retain political control.

The planters' continued dominance was not achieved
without a struggle, however. Two books on the contest for
control of the land in Georgia are Charles L. Flynn, Jr., *White
Land, Black Labor* (1983) and Steven Hahn, *The Roots of
Southern Populism: Yeoman Farmers and the Transformation
of the Georgia Up-country* (1983). The landlords' reassertion
of control over their black labor force was also contested, as
Rodney Davis's *Good and Faithful Labor: From Slavery to
Sharecropping in the Natchez District, 1860–1890* (1982) suggested and as Eric Foner argued in *Nothing But Freedom:
Emancipation and Its Legacy* (1983) and in an essay in his
Politics and Ideology in the Age of the Civil War (1979), entitled
"Reconstruction and the Crisis of Free Labor." Although the
economic system was not changed fundamentally, it was al-
tered in important ways, as several economic historians, namely

Roger Ransom and Richard Sutch, in their *One Kind of Freedom: The Economic Consequences of Emancipation* (1977), and Harold Woodman, in his "Southern Agriculture and the Law," *Agricultural History* (1979), have suggested. Harold Woodman's "Sequel to Slavery: The New History Views the Postbellum South," *Journal of Southern History* (1977) also refuted the idea, proposed by several economists using classical models, that these changes were economically rational. The new system of labor has been analyzed with great detail and insight in Gerald D. Jaynes's *Branches Without Roots: The Genesis of the Black Working Class in the American South, 1862–1882* (1986), while Barbara Fields's *Slavery and Freedom on the Middle Ground: Maryland in the Nineteenth Century* (1985) is perceptive on the postslavery system in a Border state.

After being overlooked by the Revisionists and taken for granted by the New South school, the interests and actions of the opponents of Reconstruction have been examined by historians in the past decade. Jack Maddex's *The Virginia Conservatives, 1867–1879* (1970) and George H. Thompson's *Reconstruction in Arkansas* (1976) studied them at the state level. Dan Carter examined in depth the former Confederates who secured control under Andrew Johnson's plan for the South in his *When the War Was Over: The Failure of Self-Reconstruction in the South, 1865–1867* (1985). In his *The Road to Redemption: Southern Politics, 1869–1879* (1984), which analyzed the political system of the entire region, Michael Perman paid particular attention to explaining the Democrats' strategies for regaining power as well as the internal divisions within the party. The Democrats' employment of violence as a political weapon has been examined by Allen Trelease's study of the Ku Klux Klan, entitled *White Terror* (1971), and by George Rable's *But There Was No Peace* (1984), which focussed on the more organized and overt violence of the mid-1870s. The efforts of the United States army to counter this insurgency had been analyzed earlier by James Sefton's *The United States Army and Reconstruction, 1865–1877* (1967), to which Joseph

Dawson III added a more detailed study at the state level with his *Army Generals and Reconstruction: Louisiana, 1862–1877* (1982). Finally, the existence of powerful agrarian forces within the resurgent Democratic party of the late 1870s has been noted in James T. Moore's "Redeemers Reconsidered: Change and Continuity in the Democratic South, 1870–1900," *Journal of Southern History* (1978) as well as by Wiener, Billings, and Perman in the works already cited. By comparison, C. Vann Woodward's *Origins of the New South, 1877–1913* (1951) claimed that the Redeemers were businessmen involved in railroads and manufacturing. Their mutuality of interest with northern business leaders is disputed by Patrick J. Hearden's examination of the post-Redemption cotton mill campaign, *Independence & Empire* (1982).

Reconstruction studies by the post-Revisionists have also included investigation of developments in the northern states. Ellen DuBois's *Feminism and Suffrage* (1978) discussed the movement for women's right to vote, while David Montgomery's *Beyond Equality: Labor and the Radical Republicans, 1862–1872* (1967) also broke new ground in relating the incipient labor movement to mainstream politics. The nature of the reforms undertaken by the radical Republicans in the North as well as their declining influence in the party were analyzed in James Mohr's *The Radical Republicans in New York during Reconstruction* (1973); Felice Bonadio's *North of Reconstruction: Ohio Politics, 1865–1870* (1973); and James Mohr, editor, *Radical Republicans in the North: State Politics during Reconstruction* (1976). Several studies of the northern Democrats have also appeared, the most important being Joel Silbey's *A Respectable Minority: The Democratic Party in the Civil War Era, 1860–1868* (1977) and Jean Baker's *Affairs of Party: The Political Culture of the Northern Democrats in the Mid-nineteenth Century* (1983). Morton Keller's study of public life in late-nineteenth-century America, *Affairs of State* (1977), put Reconstruction into a national context, as did William McFeely's *Grant: A Biography* (1980).

The convergence of northern and southern racial attitudes

was delineated in George Fredrickson's *The Black Image in the White Mind: The Debate over Afro-American Character and Destiny, 1871–1914* (1971) as well as in C. Vann Woodward's "Seeds of Failure in Radical Race Policy," an essay in his *American Counterpoint: Slavery and Racism in the North-South Dialogue* (1976). Woodward's critical stance toward the Republicans, which was compatible with the trend in post-Revisionist interpretation, had been expressed earlier in his analysis of the Compromise of 1877, entitled *Reunion and Reaction: The Compromise of 1877 and the End of Reconstruction* (1951). In the 1970s, the details of that deal were scrutinized and Woodward's viewpoint revised by Allan Peskin's "Was there a Compromise of 1877?" *Journal of American History* (1973); Keith Polakoff's *The Politics of Inertia: The Election of 1876 and the End of Reconstruction* (1973); George Rable's "Southern Interests and the Election of 1876: A Reappraisal," *Civil War History* (1980); and Les Benedict's "Southern Democrats in the Crisis of 1876–1877: A Reconsideration of *Reunion and Reaction*," *Journal of Southern History* (1980).

INDEX